FOUNDATIONS OF PSYCHODRAMA: HISTORY, THEORY, AND PRACTICE
THIRD EDITION

Adam Blatner, M.D., is the Director of Pediatric Consultation–Liaison Services at the Bingham Child Guidance Clinic and an assistant professor of child psychiatry at the University of Louisville School of Medicine, both in Louisville, Kentucky. He is also a board-certified trainer of psychodrama. He received his B.A. from the University of California at Berkeley in 1959 and his M.D. from the University of California Medical Center in San Francisco. His specialty training included an adult and child psychiatric residency at the Stanford University Medical Center in Palo Alto, CA, and at the Cedars-Sinai Medical Center in Los Angeles. Dr. Blatner was in the U.S. Air Force at its regional hospital in England as the medical director of its child psychiatry service. On returning to California in 1972, he began private practice in the San Francisco Bay area. Prior to his present position, he was on the staff of the Menninger Foundation in Topeka, Kansas. He is the author of several books and articles on the subject of psychodrama and its applications, including *Acting-In* (1973).

Allee Blatner studied theater performance and fine arts at the University of Texas at Austin and graphic design at Carnegie-Mellon University in Pittsburgh, PA. She has worked professionally in a variety of areas in the graphic design field. In addition, her training includes dance, creative dramatics, music, and radio/television production. Mrs. Blatner co-leads workshops for adults on cultivating imagination and spontaneity, the subject of one of her and her husband's recent books, *The Art of Play* (1987). She is also a trained auxiliary in psychodrama and co-author with her husband on other writings in this field.

FOUNDATIONS OF PSYCHODRAMA

HISTORY, THEORY, AND PRACTICE

Third Edition

Adam Blatner, M.D.
with **Allee Blatner**

SPRINGER PUBLISHING COMPANY
New York

Springer Publishing Company, Inc.
536 Broadway
New York, NY 10012

92 / 5 4 3 2

Library of Congress Cataloging-in-Publication Data

Blatner, Adam.
  Foundations of psychodrama.
  Bibliography: p.
  Includes index.
  1. Psychodrama. I. Blatner, Allee. II. Title.
[DNLM: 1. Psychodrama. WM 430.5.P8 B644f]
RC489.P7B46 1988   616.89'1523   87-26503
ISBN 0-8261-6040-9

Printed in the United States of America

Contents

PART IV Social Foundations

PART V Practical Foundations

Introduction

Psychodrama and its related methods are designed to cultivate and utilize creativity in psychotherapy, education, and other contexts. Its does this by combining the power of imagination, flexibility of drama, stimulation of action, and insights of modern psychodynamic psychology.

Also, psychodrama is unique among the psychotherapies in its capacity to address the widest range of issues: past, present, and future; intrapsychic, interpersonal, and group dynamics; support, education, expression, and insight; imagination and reality; emotions and cognition; spiritual, artistic, playful, and political aspects; prevention, diagnosis, and treatment; nonverbal communications; setting and props; and time for warming-up.

I am aware of no other field with so holistic an approach. The range of action itself has primary therapeutic value, for by addressing so many facets of existence, psychodrama suggests to patients a level of respect—the opposite of reductionism—that says, in effect (paraphrasing Walt Whitman), "Do you contradict yourself? Very well then, you contradict yourself! You are great! You contain multitudes!" The philosophy of psychodrama entails a view of people as capable of a magnificent creative process, a celebration of scores of roles—some becoming synthesized, others refined; some renegotiated, others relinquished; new ones, old ones; rigid, crystallized ones, new flexible ones; roles *in potentia*, roles foisted upon one; roles consciously chosen, roles habitually or compulsively enacted. Psychodrama's goal, like those of the other psychodynamic therapies, is the development of that part of the psyche that could be called the "choosing self," which orchestrates this multifarious existence in the service of growth, constructive social participation, and long-term, "whole-some" pleasure.

The inventor of psychodrama, J. L. Moreno, M.D., recognized that an essential component of creativity is the phenomenon of spontaneity, and activities that promote this quality serve to foster personal and interpersonal freedom and responsibility. The "drama" in psychodrama refers not to theatricality but rather to the aspect of role flexibility and the idea that we can rework our lives as if they were dramatic situations and we were playwrights. It is an extension of the idea of understanding ourselves and our social structures, and in this respect it shares the spirit of analytical approaches; in addition, it combines a method of empowerment, of responsible action in creating new possibilities. Thus, psychodrama should not be thought of as encouraging extravagant, histrionic, or artificial behavior—these are elements more properly associated with the traditional theater, movies, or television shows. Practitioners do not need to have theatrical training. Psychodramatic approaches are aimed at effective ways for generating more workable solutions to everyday problems. Indeed, many of the techniques derived from psychodrama have already become integrated into the practice of eclectic psychotherapists. Knowing about the theoretical principles underlying their use allows for a more systematic and rationally grounded approach in therapy.

The scope and power of the principles and implications of psychodrama and its related approaches may seem expansive, even somewhat grandiose. This is because they are imbued with an excitement about ways to transcend the boundaries of specialized disciplines. They offer an invigorating opportunity for promoting more inclusive, harmonious, and creative interpersonal/intergroup relations.

Appreciating the implications of these ideas may be heightened by including the intuitive and emotional as well as intellectual faculties. The fullest understanding of psychodramatic concepts requires a re-owning of the parts of the psyche that tend to be exuberant, animated, imaginative, playful, and adventurous. These are mature elements of "the inner child." Psychodrama seeks to redeem the healthy potentials to be found in the natural tendencies toward exhibitionism, omnipotence, regression, and acting out. Psychodynamic psychologies have tended to focus on the pathological expressions of these qualities, and as a result, the terms have negative connotations. However, Moreno recognized that they are inherent psychic dimensions and potential sources of creative energy that can be cultivated and transformed into personally and socially constructive channels. In addition, he saw that playful fun could also become integrated as a motivating factor in more serious tasks.

THE AUDIENCE FOR THIS BOOK

The classical approach for the training of psychotherapists who want to become practitioners of psychodrama is an unusually challenging discipline to master. It requires arduous training and a temperament that relishes working within a context of spontaneity. It is an undertaking that is clearly not for everyone. The goal of my own work as a teacher of psychodrama is to encourage a wider range of people to learn and utilize some of the methods while at the same time rediscovering a greater level of vitality available to us all. If one skill could be learned by everyone, I want it to be role reversal—to be able to see things from another's point of view (which does not mean always agreeing with that point of view). The ability to role-reverse fosters a way of being in the world that offers the potential for co-creating understanding, conflict clarification, and resolution. Each of us can learn and actively practice it in our daily lives, and thereby teach others to use it.

Psychodrama in its broadest sense includes a variety of related approaches: a dynamic and action-oriented method of individual, family, and group psychotherapy; techniques that can enrich other schools of therapy; use of structured experiences and role playing; involvement of the creative arts therapies more directly in psychotherapy, not just for analysis but for evoking spontaneity, sublimation, and metaphorical syntheses; using sociodrama and sociometry to deal with role conflicts in groups and organizations; and applying these methods in a variety of contexts. Thus, the audience for this book includes the following:

- Psychotherapists who are interested in broadening their reservoir of therapeutic approaches with the help of a clear rationale and a variety of specific suggestions.

- Those who wish to learn empathic skills in a systematic fashion, find ideas for helping in working with others, or apply these skills in training, supervision, or consultation.
- Students and practitioners of psychodrama and drama therapy who seek to discover a theoretical basis for their work, as well as inspiration and insight into its implications.
- Other creative arts therapists who want to integrate psychodramatic approaches with art, poetry, music, dance, and the like.
- Teachers and educators who already use role playing, simulations, creative drama, or experiential approaches.
- Managers, specialists in organizational development, directors of inservice training, or facilitators of community action who are able to utilize these principles with their groups.
- Innovators and students in the field of drama who are searching for ways to revitalize their art form, develop their own inner resources, and explore new pathways.
- Pastoral counselors and religious educators who are concerned with finding ways of helping people relate to spiritual issues in a more personally meaningful fashion.
- "People helpers," including nurses, social workers, leaders of self-help groups, camp counselors, hospice volunteers, and recreation workers who want to develop their skills in promoting group cohesion, spontaneity, and creativity in their activities.

In other everyday contexts these approaches have applications for those who want to help friends, resolve conflicts with co-workers or committee members, and bring better strategies into the more personal roles of relating to family members.

Psychodramatic methods, in this broader sense, may be thought of as tools—a psychosocial technology for helping people relate to one another more effectively and harmoniously. The goal of this approach is not only to help individuals but ultimately to be put to work in healing the divisions between groups and nations.

THE PLAN OF THE BOOK

An overview begins in the form of a brief description of the psychodramatic method which offers an introductory orientation to those who are relatively unfamiliar with it. This is followed by the first part, which presents the historical foundations of psycho-drama. The origins of psychodrama are rooted in the interdisciplinary and multifaceted interests of its inventor, J. L. Moreno, and the emphasis here is on directing the reader's attention to his philosophy and social vision. After discussing the later developments in the field, we present the factors that have affected the recognition and utilization of psychodramatic methods.

The second part explores some of the philosophical foundations of psychodrama, again with an intention to communicate the spirit behind the use of these methods as well as suggest wider potentials for their application. These aspects are especially noteworthy to psychotherapists because they are rarely noted in psychiatric textbooks.

The third part grounds the psychodramatic method in a foundation of psychological theory, using a rational framework that Allee Blatner and I have developed and call role dynamics. The theory of role dynamics has the potential for integrating the best of the other theories of psychology and psychotherapy, and as such it also serves as a basis for appreciating the creative arts therapies. Some practical applications of role dynamics are also presented.

The fourth part explores the interpersonal dimension of Moreno's ideas, looking at role dynamics from the viewpoint of his method of sociometry. Far more than technique is involved here: There is a way of thinking about relationships that has tremendous implications for making social psychology a matter of clinical and everyday relevance.

The fifth part presents the theory behind the various techniques, emphasizing again the principle involved in fostering creativity. An extensive listing and glossary of the various techniques follows. The book ends with a bibliography of the major works related to psychodrama that have appeared in the last 15 years and an appendix that describes a chronology of historical events relating to psychodrama and group psychotherapy.

ABOUT THE PRESENT EDITION

This volume is an extensively revised and expanded version of a monograph we produced privately in 1985, and it is meant to serve as a complement to my earlier book, *Acting-In: Practical Applications of Psychodramatic Methods* (New York: Springer Publishing Company, 1973, 2nd edition, 1989). Although a number of other books on psychodrama have appeared, the implicit philosophy and theoretical foundations of the subject must be developed further. This book makes a contribution toward that goal in a more systematic fashion.

The theories presented here are not meant to be a restatement of Moreno's writings. I have freely modified, expanded, and added to his ideas, in full awareness that I might not be presenting them as he would. It is my hope that this book will improve access to and understanding of psychodramatic methods based on my own study and work over the last 20 years. In honoring the creative act as more valuable than what Moreno called the "cultural conserve," the products of the creative act, I invite you as the reader to respond to this material with your own ideas—to use this book as a catalyst for your own exploration, personally and professionally, with these approaches. In addition, I would be delighted to receive your comments, criticisms, and suggestions.

ADAM BLATNER
with ALLEE BLATNER
Louisville, Kentucky
August, 1987

To Zerka Toeman Moreno,
with gratitude and deep respect
for capturing the essence of psychodrama,
adding her own insights,
and communicating these to others

1

An Overview
of Psychodrama

Psychodrama is a method of psychotherapy in which patients enact the relevant events in their lives instead of simply talking about them. This involves exploring in action not only historical events but, more importantly, dimensions of psychological events not ordinarily addressed in conventional dramatic process: unspoken thoughts, encounters with those not present, portrayals of fantasies of what others might be feeling and thinking, envisioning future possibilities, and many other aspects of the phenomenology of human experience. Although psychodrama is usually used in a group setting and can be a very useful method to catalyze group process (and in turn be catalyzed by the group dynamics), it should not be thought of as being essentially a form of group psychotherapy. It may be used, as it is in 'France, with several trained co-therapists and a single patient. Psychodrama may also be used with families or even, in a modified form, in individual psychotherapy.

Psychodrama was originated in 1921 by Jacob L. Moreno, M.D.

(1889–1974) as an approach that was integrated in his mind with a vision of interactive group dynamics and a philosophy of creativity, all of which were refined over the next few decades. It is important to recognize Moreno's work because his ideas about the essence of healing of both individuals and communities have continuing relevance today. Many of his methods have been incorporated into other approaches to psychotherapy, as well as into sociology, group dynamics, research, and other areas, yet their theoretical foundations are often overlooked.

Psychodrama can refer to both a specific therapeutic method and also the use of a wider variety of techniques that have applications in therapy, business, and education, as well as in many other areas. In addition, there are theoretical principles that may be used to address the needs of a broad spectrum of issues. In this sense, psychodrama is analogous to the way psychoanalysis is both a specific technique of treatment and an orientation to dynamic depth psychology. Also, as with psychoanalysis, the various frontiers of psychodrama branch into the fields of sociology, the arts, ethics, education, recreation, and the humanities. The term "psychodrama" as used in this book will refer to a variety of activities, such as simple role playing in individual or family therapy, the use of structured experiences in groups, and other examples. More formal enactments will be clearly designated "classical psychodrama."

BASIC ELEMENTS

Aside from the many techniques, Moreno said there were five basic elements in classical psychodrama:

- The protagonist, who is usually the patient.
- The director, who is usually the therapist.
- The auxiliary, a role played by either a co-therapist or another patient who helps the protagonist explore the enactment.
- The audience, usually consisting of other patients or staff members not directly involved in the enactment.
- The stage, which in most cases is simply a space in a room large enough for some physical movement, perhaps 50 to 79 sq ft in area.

The reasons Moreno chose to use dramaturgical terms instead of simply calling these roles "patient" or "therapist" are discussed further in Chapter 15 under the headings of the specific terms involved.

SOME TYPICAL ENACTMENTS

A fuller appreciation of the nature of psychodrama can best be gathered by considering a variety of scenes that might be enacted in psychotherapy. The following vignettes will supply some examples. In order to clarify the meaning of a complex family interaction, the patient (or "protagonist," in psychodramatic terminology) presents his family situation in an improvised dramatic enactment. He first sets up the physical scene—say, breakfast in the dining room. Others in the group may be selected to play the various family members, thus serving as "auxiliaries" to the patient. The protagonist demonstrates a little of each family member's behavior, including nonverbal styles of communication and a few typical sentences, or at least some (fantasized) inner thoughts about the situation. Then the auxiliaries take the role designated, and when the whole scene is established, the director has the family begin to act in the manner suggested. The patient is transported back in time, as it were, and begins to interact with his various family members as if the scene were occurring in the present moment, in the here-and-now.

During this enactment, the director might have the patient change parts ("role-reverse") with one after another of his family members, portraying on a deeper level the feelings of these figures. In the role-reversed positions, the patient is encouraged to sense into and experience empathically what that point of view might be like. (It is therapeutic to go beyond the patient's tendency to caricature others if possible.) Other dramatic potentials are also made available, such as having the patient express as fully as possible, in action if indicated, the feelings aroused in the encounter. (Usually only one or two significant others become the focus of the enactment as time goes on.) Alternatively, he might enact a subscene in which the other person behaves in the most desired or helpful way, which often brings out the subconscious needs in the relationship. He might play the ideal father, for example, and then, having modeled it, allow the auxiliary to play that role while he experiences being fathered in the way he always secretly wanted.

Another enactment might be the exploration of a dream, also with the goal of increased self-awareness or insight. The protagonist begins with a brief statement of the dream as if it were happening in the present moment. Then she enacts the dream in slightly more detail. To deepen the experience, figures in the dream are explored by having the protagonist take the role of each one. The director "warms up" this role-taking by interviewing the protagonist in the role of the dream figure, whether that figure is a person, such as the protagonist's mother; an inanimate object, such as the bridge they find themselves walking across; or even something more amorphous, such as the growing darkness of the scene. All aspects of the dream are treated as if they were a part of the psyche trying to express some aspect of the protagonist's inner self and/or existential dilemma.

As with the previous example, part of the psychodrama might be to "dream the dream onward" (in the words of the analytical psychologist James Hillman). In the involved state of spontaneity, the protagonist is allowed to project her sense of what happens next and what happens after that. Other people, in their roles as auxiliaries, play the various dream characters or objects, and the protagonist in the mild trance of the moment co-directs the event as it unfolds in her imagination. If the action tends to reinforce the patient's pathology, the director might replay the ending, working mutually with her, in order to choose a more positive outcome. Alternatively, the roots of the negative outcome might be explored by the therapist by interviewing the protagonist in the role of one of the other dream figures. The goal is to bring to the surface as many of the hidden assumptions as possible without intellectualizing about it and then to open the protagonist's mind to co-creating alternative options.

A third example would be the clarification of a patient's goals using the technique of future projection. This consolidates the therapeutic alliance and develops the patient's sense of responsibility. Instead of talking about a situation, which makes it too easy to distance the self from the real issues, the patient is instructed to become involved as if the situation is happening in the present moment. The challenge of setting up scenes according to the heart's desire brings out layers of inhibition and evasion, and yet the physical action required gently moves past these defenses because, after all, the protagonist is simply making explicit his own choices. For some patients, simply doing this is enough. For others, playing these scenes helps make them more realistic. It also tests the scene's feasibility, a form of confrontation that shifts the point of frustration from other people, who would become invested with negative qualities, to the neutral demands of the situation. In other words, for those who tend to feel oppressed or unfairly treated, it is not the judgment of any authority that accounts for an inadequate performance but the requirements of the role, which then evokes the function of reality testing.

Another possible type of scene offers an opportunity for patients to access subconscious desires and give themselves corrective emotional experiences. Unhappy or even traumatic scenes can be enacted, the final scene being one in which the protagonist creates a more positive outcome, a happy ending. This can involve not only active mastery but also a receptive experience of being empathized with, held, comforted, encouraged, or appreciated, as mentioned in the first example when the auxiliary plays the ideal father.

A fifth example for a psychodramatic enactment would be the exploration of a better alternative strategy, a rehearsal, so to speak. Whether anticipating a date, an interview for a job, a confrontation with a co-worker, or the challenge of disciplining a child, this role playing technique has become a major part of behavior therapy, assertion training, and other eclectic approaches. The patient is enabled to replay the scene until a modicum of success is achieved, in addition to having other group members show how they would deal with the situation (i.e., modeling), getting feedback, and, most importantly, receiving encouragement. Patients can practice self-expression if they are too inhibited, and self-control (with active but calm behavioral responses) if they tend to be histrionic or explosive.

A sixth type of scene involves the use of psychodramatic methods to help a patient cope with a hallucination. Of course, the application of these techniques requires clinical judgment. The patient is helped to portray the hallucination in concrete form, with its accompanying nonverbal components—tone of voice, pace, intensity, phraseology. Alternatively, an auxiliary might play the role of the hallucination. The source of the hallucination can be amplified, explicitly projected, and externalized, the role-taking being similar to that described above for working with dream figures. This character can then be interviewed, and a negotiating encounter might even lead to some modification of the hallucination's power. When the situation is judiciously chosen, this action will not strengthen the psychotic process because the active engagement with these mechanisms introduces a measure of voluntary control that tends to neutralize some of the sense of victimization.

As a seventh example, unresolved mourning of any person, pet, place, part of the body, social role, or other loss can be worked through in a "good-bye encounter," exploring the concrete images and role-reversing with the lost object. The dialogue that ensues may be directed toward a healthy internalization. In a similar sense, this approach may be useful in resolving unfinished or unexpressed conflict with someone in the present or recent past, the other people being played by auxiliaries or empty chairs.

An enacted encounter may also be the vehicle for understanding the other person(s), discovering the depth of one's own feelings, receiving validation for the (at least partial) plausibility of one's own positions, or discovering a more effective strategy for working out the problem, as well as other possible goals. Using auxiliaries to play parts of the self (the "double" technique) may help express feelings more clearly. Other roles patients can experience include explorations of confused or unclear feeling states, or learning how to understand significant others (through role reversal, of course). The menu of possible scenes for exploration is extensive, perhaps limited only by the imagination of the director. Other scenes and techniques will be discussed further at the end of the book, and references that describe the flow of events are noted in the Bibliography.

PSYCHODRAMATIC TECHNIQUES IN PSYCHOTHERAPY

One of the most important aspects of psychodramatic methods is that they may be applied as specific techniques to facilitate the process of individual, couple, family, group, or milieu therapy. For example, it is particularly useful to teach patients how to do role reversal as a way of enhancing empathy and more mature communications. This technique is also helpful in resolving conflicts.

Another technique that is a powerful adjunct to therapy is that of the double, which may be used by the therapist as a way to communicate empathic understanding, elaboration, and a kind of interpretation while yet working within the patient's "self-system" (as Carl Rogers termed it). This reduces the tendencies toward resistance in the one-to-one work between a patient and a therapist, with its inevitable gradient of power.

By including a third (and perhaps even a fourth) person in the session, and having these people play a variety of roles—witnesses, advocates, doubles, and especially auxiliaries—therapists can use small-group dynamics in a creatively flexible fashion. The auxiliaries can function as assistants in helping a patient do mini-enactments or encounters, and the figures in a patient's life (such as the patient's mother, father, spouse, or employer) then can engage the patient with more vigor, thus evoking from the patient more spontaneous emotional reactions.

Other techniques, such as "asides," role playing, "the mirror," or having patients play multiple parts of themselves in different chairs, may all bring out aspects of a situation that are hard to get at in ordinary, verbal forms of therapy.

RELATED APPROACHES

Psychodrama is one of a number of related approaches, and it may be helpful to differentiate it for purposes of noting the variety of applications. Each of the following has a place in the overall treatment repertoire, and often the actual use of the methods may involve elements from several approaches.

Role playing as a type of psychodramatic work refers more to the task of finding the best behavioral response to a situation. The techniques of enactment, replay, modeling by other group members, and coaching are most relevant. In practice, there are many who choose to use the term "role playing" to refer to modified or regular psychodrama or sociodrama, in part because in some settings the "psycho-" or the "-drama" have unpleasant or misleading connotations.

Sociodrama refers to a psychodramatic exploration of the problems inherent in a role relationship, apart from the other role-dimension specifics of the people involved. Thus, a sociodrama of mothers and daughters might explore a variety of important aspects of expectations, historical changes, beliefs, and motives that are involved in this relationship. Similarly, one could produce sociodramas involving encounters between policemen and young people, blacks and whites, Catholics and Protestants, men and women, and so on. In contrast, psychodrama refers to the situations engendered by the convergence of multiple role relationships, such as a particular young, black, married, woman police officer in a particular relationship with her daughter, involving issues of temperament, specific age-appropriate issues, a husband with such-and-such qualities, and so on.

Drama therapy refers to the utilization of drama and dramatic methods in group situations, usually for the general purposes of heightening awareness of psychological issues, developing skills of improvisation and creative thinking, expanding the role repertoire to include body movement and other aesthetic dimensions, and similar approaches. In its earlier stage of development, drama therapy involved helping patients to put on conventional plays or musicals. However, since the late 1960s, the influences of Moreno's ideas about improvisation, the British approach to "remedial drama," and the growth of improvisational theater and comedy in the United States have combined to shift the drama therapy approach more toward the theme of utilizing spontaneity.

Theater games may be used as warm-ups for both psychodrama groups and drama therapy groups, although they may be amplified in the latter setting. Drama therapists sometimes do psychodrama as a way of following up on the material that comes out of a particularly evocative warm-up.

Psychodramatic methods are particularly useful, as they can be integrated into more conventional approaches in individual, family, group, and milieu therapy. Indeed, many of Moreno's techniques have become integrated into other schools. Fritz Perls adopted the vehicle of the "empty chair" in Gestalt therapy (adding many ideas that deserve to be learned by psychodramatists and other therapists). Virginia Satir incorporated the psychodramatic technique called the action sociogram, relabeling it "family sculpture." Nowadays, family therapists behave in a distinctly directorial fashion, and in some ways training in active family therapy is closer to psychodrama training than the training of conventional (psychoanalytically oriented, relatively passive) group therapists.

Guided fantasy or imagery work often uses principles of psychodrama, especially in constructively addressing situations as they arise in the imaginal interpersonal/intrapsychic context. Hypnotherapists can also adapt these strategies for exploring alternatives. For example, in neurolinguistic programming, a modified hypnotherapeutic approach, one technique recently used at a workshop was that of dividing the self into different parts and having them encounter each other or interact in other ways. Eric Berne's use of different ego states in his method of Transactional Analysis also involved a kind of dividing the self into its components, the better to have them negotiate new arrangements. In this sense, Virginia Satir's idea of a "parts party" also is an example of the psychodramatic technique, the "multiple parts of the self."

Action techniques involve the use of structured experiences for warming up a group, practicing a skill, exploring an issue, or working through a conflict. Often these would supplement or even bypass intellectual approaches, thus engaging more of the person's abilities. The human potential movement of the late 1960s and early 1970s might be thought of as a synthesis of the ideas of humanistic psychology, existential psychology, group dynamics (itself in part derived from Moreno's work), and a variety of action techniques taken from psychodrama and other approaches. The primarily verbal approach to the encounter group became more experiential in the work of such innovators as Will Schutz at the Esalen Institute. Since then, many new eclectic approaches to psychotherapy have emerged, and many therapists are increasingly integrating techniques that use psychodrama, imagery, manipulation or exercises of the body, reevaluation of cognitions, and behavioristic approaches, all manifestations of a more active approach to treatment.

It should be noted that, although the application of psychodramatic methods is relatively easy, the processes of coordinating them in a more intensive formal psychodrama requires extensive training. Psychodrama can be a very powerful tool, and real clinical judgment is needed, as well as arrangements for follow-up. Indeed, psychodrama might be thought of as the surgery of psychotherapy, a process that can be catalytic but requires a kind of "postoperative" access to professionals for the working-through and integration of the action insights.

In summary, the process of psychodrama is enormously complex because of the many facets of life that it can address and manipulate. On the other hand, its essence is relatively simple: Help the patient experience his or her situation as vividly as possible; help unspoken thoughts be expressed; help group members to help each other; help patients to develop and apply their own creativity to their life challenges. Psychodrama is a broad group of methodologies that facilitates the principles of dynamic psychotherapy.

PART I
Historical Foundations

2

The Historical Origins of Psychodrama

The roots of psychodrama actually involve an integrated system of philosophical, sociological, and psychological theories developed by J. L. Moreno, M.D. To understand them it is important to know about the themes that dominated most of his thinking and activities. A chronology of many of the key events in Moreno's life (Appendix A) should enhance this understanding. As an introductory overview, however, consider that Moreno's work is an effort at synthesizing the following principles:

- An existential, phenomenological, and process-oriented philosophy, one that emphasizes the importance of creativity.
- The nature of spontaneity, its value, and ways for developing it as a key to becoming more creative.
- More authentic interpersonal relationships, fostered by methods for promoting encounter, feedback, and collective social change.

- Improvisational theater as a vehicle for revitalizing the arts and as a source of "mass therapy."
- Methods for research and further applications for these principles.

These themes were reflected in Moreno's varied roles in his early career in the second and third decades of his life in Vienna (1908–1925):

- student of philosophy/spirituality
- field worker in child development and creative dramatics
- medical student and practicing physician
- applied social psychologist and sociologist
- editor of a literary journal
- director of improvisational theater

What unites these varied pursuits is a central philosophical idea. Moreno (1947) wrote:

> I suffered from an idee fixe . . . [it] became my constant source of productivity; it proclaimed that there is a sort of primordial nature which is immortal and returns afresh with every generation, a first universe which contains all beings and in which all events are sacred. I liked that enchanting realm and did not plan to leave it, ever. (p. 3)

The primordial nature Moreno writes of is an attempt to describe a class of meta-archetypal processes, basic patterns of creative action that give impetus to the relationships we call the laws of nature. This metaphysical intuition reveals a theme that connects his work with Jung, Rank, Assagioli, the implications of modern quantum physics, and some esoteric philosophies of the past, especially the neoplatonic ideas within the Kabbalah, the Jewish mystical tradition (Blatner, in press).

Moreno was suggesting that there are realms that give form to our own plane of material existence—insubstantial yet influential creative patterns that precede or are implicit in, yet not restricted to, any actual event. From a psychological standpoint, this suggests a source in the psyche that functions as an unending fountain of imagery, vitality, and freedom. The reason he called this realm sacred is that he experienced this dimension as being close to the essential nature of divinity, of his conceptualization of God as a creative force. This was not only a creation at the beginning of time, nor one that determines the course of action in every event, but rather the force of imminent activity itself. Yet it was totally decentralized, operating through whatever degrees of freedom are available to every being, every atom, cell, butterfly, or poet. In this sense, God excites, persuades, invites, but does not control or coerce. To be more precise, this archetypal action returns afresh not in every generation but rather in every moment.

Moreno intended to remain in contact with this "enchanting realm" because the essential creativity available there has the power to enliven our existence, further our growth, and connect us with our spiritual source. The theme of creativity, viewed as a metaphysical and theological principle, carries a moral imperative far stronger than if it was merely a psychological phenomenon: It was the foundation of his approach to applied existentialism and unifies his writings on sociometry, group psychotherapy, psychodrama, the arts, and culture in general. He always sought to transcend mere technique and to widen the goals and potentials of his work beyond the boundaries of professional disciplines.

Viewed from this perspective, another philosophical inspiration motivated his choice of the drama as a vehicle for exploring what he termed "axiodramatic" questions of ultimate value:

> . . . no one can play in a materialistic age the roles of gods and saints without getting the slur of madness or criminality thrown at their heads. The theatre was a safe retreat for unsuspected revolution and offered unlimited possibilities for spontaneity research on the experimental level. (Moreno, 1947, p. 6)

This statement illuminates Moreno's personality, his enormous vitality, willingness to take risks, capacity for enjoyment, and adventurousness into realms of creativity. Yet, knowing the world to be a co-creative process, his goal was not for his own personal spiritual elevation. Like the legendary bodhisattva of the Buddhist tradition and with a sentiment similar to the ideas of Teilhard de Chardin, Moreno wanted to help the whole world to use methods of encounter and group dynamics, to help all people develop their own creativity and thus move toward a more harmonious future. As mentioned in the Introduction, these ideas are best appreciated when you open to the most expansive, visionary part of yourself and allow your own enthusiasm and optimism to have free rein.

BIOGRAPHICAL BACKGROUND

Jacob Moreno Levi was born on May 18, 1889, in Bucharest, Romania, the oldest of six children, three boys and three girls. He changed his name to Jacob Levi Moreno when he came to America. He was the son of a Sephardic Jewish family (the Sephardic Jews were those who emigrated to other parts of the Mediterranean area after being forced out of Spain at the end of the 15th century). It should be noted that Moreno stated in error in some of his writings that he was born in 1892 on a ship sailing in the Black Sea. The corrected date is based on the record of his birth in the city archives (Bratescu, 1975).

The common thread in all of Moreno's diverse endeavors is the continuing expression of vitality and creativity, not bound to the forms he devised but to the spirit permeating his work and leading him onward. This was present from early in his life. As a child he lived in his family's home, which was located across the street from a church in Bucharest. It seems probable that his play experiences included children of other faiths, and perhaps he began to explore religious images as a way of making ecumenical bridges with those playmates.

Moreno's philosophy was influenced by an "axiodramatic" episode. (Axiodrama refers to enactments in which the central issues involve ethical, religious, or cosmological themes.) This event also stimulated his awareness of the importance of the child's strivings for self-expression (Moreno, 1946). One day when he was 4 1/2 years old, young Jacob was playing with some neighborhood children in the enormous cellar of his home. His parents had gone out. Jacob suggested they play God and His angels, and he volunteered to play God. First, they proceeded to construct a heaven out of the chairs in the house, stacking them in a pyramid upon a large table, tying the chairs' legs together, and finally helping Jacob to the top seat, near the ceiling of the basement. This accomplished, the other children began to circle the structure, flapping their arms as angel wings. One called out to Jacob to join in the make-believe flying, and in his absorption in the play, he jumped from his throne, fell, and broke his arm. The experience impressed him with the need for children to have opportunities for symbolic gratification of even their most grandiose fantasies.

One of the axioms of psychohistory is that the theoretical biases of innovators in psychology, philosophy, and other fields have been influenced by their childhood experiences. For example, it has been suggested that Freud's early development occurred in a family setting that would naturally exaggerate oedipal dynamics; Adler needed to compensate for feelings of inferiority due to a short stature caused by childhood rickets; Jung evolved a psychology that could explain in part his own mystical experiences; and Rank's emphasis on the creative aspects of the therapeutic process reflected his own background as an artist. In addition, psychohistorians claim that the therapeutic method or technique that accompanies a new theory also reflects the originator's personal style. In light of the stories he tells about himself, Moreno's dramatic interests could be traced to what he called the healthy megalomania of his childhood play.

When Moreno was 6 years of age his family moved to Vienna, Austria. His languages had been Romanian and Ladino (a derivative of Spanish written in the Hebrew script, just as Yiddish is a derivative of German written in the Hebrew script), but in Vienna he learned German (Johnson, 1959). Little is known of his life between the move and when he became a student of philosophy, theology, and mathematics at the University of Vienna. The nature of children's play caught his interest around 1908, and he observed their activities in the parks around the city. In addition, he would tell the children stories, which they would enact; and he noticed that when they had no scripts, their portrayals of the roles would be more vital and spontaneous. The importance of spontaneity began to form as a significant concept in his consciousness. It led to his experimentation with various kinds of improvisatory dramatics with the children (and sometimes their parents) in the Augarten and other parks in Vienna. By 1911 he had organized a theater of spontaneity for children.

Among other studies at this time, Moreno was interested in comparative religion and the achievements of the various religious and philosophical leaders. His "effort to transcend and supersede them all" reflects the goal of any creative philosopher who attempts to contribute something else, something in addition to and improving on the work of those who have gone before. Moreno co-created a group of young spiritual enthusiasts who were active, although they shared no formal religious observances: "We all wore beards, we never stood still, walked, walked, walked, stopped everyone we encountered along the way, shook hands and talked to them. We were all poor but we shared whatever we had, our poverty" (Moreno, 1972, p. 208). Clearly influenced by the emergence of early existentialist thought, possibly through the work of Dostoyevsky and Nietzsche, as well as some of the writers in central Europe, he and his friends were attempting to put it into action, to live the spirit of creativity in everyday life.

One influence on Moreno was the then popular philosophy of Henri Bergson, who wrote that the process of creativity was central to the essence of reality. Moreno felt a need to add his own modification to Bergson's ideas by emphasizing that the moment is a "revolutionary category" that holds the potential for creative action (Moreno, 1971b). He began to write about creativity as an essential feature of the Divine Nature, in contrast to traditional ideas that spoke about God as "out there" making judgments.

Around 1910, Moreno began to formulate the idea that the divine force, or "Godhead," was not just a distant creator but an ongoing active principle expressed through the beingness and spontaneity of all creatures. Over the next 7 years he wrote about his own metaphysical concepts in a series of philosophical discourses. These extended Bergson's views on creativity to emphasize the potential for the "revolutionary act" in the "here and now" (a term Moreno coined during that time). Some of Moreno's papers (published between 1909 and 1918) included "Man, the Child," "The Children's Realm," "The Godhead as Comedian," "Invitation to an Encounter," "Silence," "The Godhead as Actor," and "The Godhead as Creator" (Meiers, 1945).

In 1914 Moreno was momentously inspired and wrote a poetical work that covers most of his theological concepts, *The Words of the Father.* It was first published anonymously and later appeared under his own name. The book is a vision focused on the present and the future rather than the past. It relates to life always in terms of the possibilities for creative action in the "category of the moment." A review of the complete philosophical writings Moreno produced during these years shows that he deserves to be included among the early existentialists.

During this same period (1911–1917) Moreno was a medical student at the University of Vienna. Part of his duties involved assisting the psychiatric chief of staff, but he disagreed with the approach. Likewise, he was aware of Freud's work but felt it did nothing to help patients create new aspirations and goals. Moreno saw this as the crucial challenge in treating mental illness. An example of his attitude and manner can be found in an anecdote he frequently related:

> I met Dr. Freud only on one occasion. It occurred in 1912 when, while working at the Psychiatric Clinic in Vienna University, I attended one of his lectures. Dr. Freud had just ended his analysis

of a telepathic dream. As the students filed out he asked me what I was doing. "Well, Dr. Freud, I start where you leave off. You meet people in the artificial setting of your office, I meet them on the street and in their home, in their natural surroundings. You analyze their dreams. I try to give them the courage to dream again. I teach the people how to play God." Dr. Freud looked at me as if puzzled. (Moreno, 1946, pp. 5–6)

While in medical school, Moreno began to shift his interest in group dynamics and the importance of social integration from children to adults. For example, he learned of the exploitation and government harassment of prostitutes in Vienna. He got an idea to help them organize themselves into "self-help" groups—one of the first instances of such social organization—in 1912. The women used their meetings for both emotional support and to share constructive ideas about coping with their sociopolitical situation.

At the beginning of World War I, an Italian-Austrian refugee camp was established at Mittendorf, a suburb of Vienna, and Moreno served as a physician there. To help foster democratic and participatory behavior, he created the early elements of his method of sociometry: Instead of assigning people to various living arrangements, he used questionnaires to help them choose the people with whom they wanted to be neighbors.

It is interesting to remember that Moreno lived in Vienna during its "golden era" (1895–1920), a time when it was one of the cultural capitals of the world. He associated with the intellectuals of the city, especially the writers and philosophers. In 1917 he edited a literary journal, *Daimon*, the leading existentialist and expressionist magazine of that period. It included some of the early works of Franz Kafka, the theologian Martin Buber, and the existential philosopher Max Scheler, among others (Treadwell & Treadwell, 1972). In addition to writing inspirational, theological poetry, he also was involved in social action and wrote a small book entitled *Invitation to an Encounter*—one of the first uses of the term *encounter*—from which he often quoted this particular passage:

A meeting of two: eye to eye, face to face.
And when you are near I will tear your eyes out
and place them instead of mine,
and you will tear my eyes out
and will place them instead of yours,
and I will look at you with your eyes
and you will look at me with mine.

Moreno's philosophical ideas demanded implementation in action. This led him to the social experiments (some of which are noted above) that directly contributed to the evolution of sociometry, psychodrama, and group psychotherapy, as well as inspiring the movement toward "living theater" and improvisational dramatics (Moreno, 1971a). April 1, 1921, was the date Moreno gave as the real beginning of psychodrama. He had organized a troupe of actors (including Peter Lorre, who was later to become famous in the movies) and initiated his idea of mass therapeutics by opening an impromptu theater to present *Die Stegreiftheatre* (The Theater of Spontaneity). Actually, turning it into a therapeutic method emerged more gradually after the second or third year of experimentation. Moreno produced a variety of experimental impromptu shows, including "The Living Newspaper," in which his actors would portray the events of the daily news. In a way, this was the beginning of sociodrama (Toeman, 1949). During these years he also had a general medical practice in a suburb of Vienna named Bad Voslau. (When he returned to be honored by the town in the late 1960s, there were people who still remembered him as "our Doctor.")

In 1925, postwar Austria was chaotic and could not support Moreno's experiments in applied social science and therapeutic theater. He thought of emigrating to either Russia, with its "great new experiment," or to the United States. He chose the latter because he realized what he needed was freedom to pursue his theories. Moreno was able to go to America because he was, among other things, an inventor. He invented a wire recorder, a precursor of today's tape recorders, in an attempt to transcribe and play back process recordings of activities for exploratory and therapeutic aims. A company in America was interested enough to help him emigrate from Austria in 1925, and he settled in New York City.

When Moreno arrived in the United States, he was surprised at the popularity of psychoanalysis; back in Vienna it was still on the fringe of respectability (J. Moreno, 1985). The dominance of psychoanalysis in America presented him with an unexpected challenge. Also, he was unprepared for Americans' intolerance of eccentricity—in Europe most intellectuals were expected to be somewhat eccentric!

Despite these and other limitations, over the next 20 years Moreno produced his most innovative work. (The high points are noted in the chronicle of events in Appendix A.) Working mainly

in New York, he developed psychodrama and group psychotherapy; wrote a number of books and articles; opened his own sanitarium in Beacon, about 60 miles north of New York City; published
two professional journals, including one of his own writings, and
a number of seminal articles by other innovators in psychology,
sociology and education; organized the first professional association of group psychotherapists; and offered open psychodrama sessions in New York City that were a showcase where many professionals witnessed psychodynamic methods other than the
traditional psychoanalytic approaches. A. H. Maslow (1968), Eric
Berne (1970), and Will Schutz (1971) have all clearly acknowledged Moreno's role as a source of many of the most innovative
techniques in modern eclectic psychotherapy.

The years of refining and promoting his ideals were to follow.
From the late 1940s to his death in 1974, he and his wife, Zerka,
were tireless in their efforts to share, teach, and demonstrate the
principles of spontaneity and creativity as fundamental aspects of
the human potential. These events and Zerka's continued involvement will be discussed further in Chapter 3.

In summary, the variety of Moreno's interests and activities has
in common his devotion to the vision of a healthier world. Many
years of experience with individuals and groups convinced him
that the principles of encounter, group dynamics, action methods
in therapy, and spontaneity, in combination with the other methods he developed, were valuable and significant contributions to
psychology, sociology, and philosophy. He and Zerka spent much
time and exerted great personal energy to ensure that his work was
thrust into the evolution of psychology and the social sciences.

The unifying vision for all of his work was the active and vitaliz-
ing force of spontaneity and creativity in our lives. It was a philosophy to be lived, full of its attendant existential risks. To the extent
that he erred, it was usually because he was exploring the limits of
his own vitality and authenticity. He consciously and flamboyantly
modeled the behaviors of exploring spontaneity that he advocated.
If at times he failed to conform to the social expectations of some
of his colleagues, it was the price he was always willing to pay. For
those fortunate enough to have been with him, he was undoubt-
edly one of the most dynamic and courageous pioneers in the history of psychiatry.

REFERENCES

Berne, Eric. (1970). Letter to the editor. *American Journal of Psychiatry, 126*(10), 1520.

Blatner, Adam. (1988). Moreno's metaphysical source. *Journal of Group Psychotherapy, Psychodrama, and Sociometry,* in press.

Bratescu, Gheorgh. (1975). The date and birthplace of J. L. Moreno. *Group Psychotherapy and Psychodrama, 28,* 2–4. (*Author's note:* This birthdate is three years earlier than previously reported statements.)

Johnson, Paul E. (1959). Interpersonal psychology of religion—Moreno and Buber. *Group Psychotherapy, 12,* 211–217.

Maslow, Abraham H. (1968, August 2). Letter to the editor. *Life,* p. 15.

Meiers, Joseph. (1945). Origins and development of group psychotherapy—Historical survey. *Sociometry, 8,* 499–530.

Moreno, J. L. (1946). *Psychodrama* (Vol. 1). Beacon, NY: Beacon House.

Moreno, J. L. (1947). *The theatre of spontaneity.* Beacon, NY: Beacon House.

Moreno, J. L. (1971a). Influence of the Theater of Spontaneity upon the modern drama. *Handbook of International Sociometry, 6,* 84–90.

Moreno, J. L. (1971b). *The words of the Father.* Beacon, NY: Beacon House.

Moreno, J. L. (1972). The religion of God-Father. In Paul E. Johnson (Ed.), *Healer of the mind: A psychiatrist's search for faith* (pp. 197–215). Nashville, TN: Abingdon.

Moreno, Jonathan. (1985, January). Presentation at the Western Division conference of the American Society for Group Psychotherapy and Psychodrama, Los Angeles.

Schutz, Will. (1971). *Here comes everybody: Body-mind and encounter culture.* New York: Harper & Row.

Toeman, Zerka. (1949). History of the sociometric movement in headlines. *Sociometry, 12,* 255–259.

Treadwell, Thomas, & Treadwell, Jean. (1972). The pioneer of the group encounter movement. *Group Psychotherapy and Psychodrama, 25,* 16–26.

3

Further Developments in Psychodrama

From the late 1940s onward, the field of psychodrama matured. Along with sociometry and group psychotherapy, Moreno's work began to be applied in a variety of settings such as schools, recreation, rehabilitation programs for the developmentally disabled, the military, management, and the training of professionals from teachers to salespersons. Moreno encouraged the development of innovations in psychotherapy, and in the late 1950s, in collaboration with Frieda Fromm-Reichmann and Jules Masserman, he edited a series of books that presented some of the more novel approaches. He was especially interested in cultivating the emerging creative arts therapies; for example, the pioneer of dance therapy, Marian Chace, had one of her first articles published in Moreno's journal (Chace, 1945).

Historically, it is important to remember that group psychotherapy was an innovation that was not readily accepted by the traditional professional community. Moreno was as devoted to the development of group psychotherapy as he was to psychodrama. He wanted to emphasize the importance of psychodrama's more interactional approach; nevertheless, he initiated and helped organize a number of national and international conferences on group therapy that actively included psychoanalytically oriented leaders. These conferences offered a forum for interchange for new approaches, such as Joshua Bierer's "social clubs," Virginia Satir's family therapy, Maxwell Jones's therapeutic community, and George Vassilou's use of art therapy techniques in group psychotherapy.

Moreno functioned as an important ongoing catalyst for innovation and eclecticism in psychotherapy, especially during a time when alternative approaches were having difficulty gaining acceptance in the clinical professions, then under the domination of psychoanalysis. His writings and public demonstration sessions in New York influenced Fritz Perls, who had recently arrived from South Africa. Several of the pioneers of the encounter group movement published some of their earliest experiments in Moreno's journal, *Sociatry.*

Several family members contributed to Moreno's successful efforts. Among others, his first wife, Florence, was active in education and child development and helped his work on spontaneity theory and psychodrama. (They had a daughter, Regina, born in 1939.) Financial assistance was given by his younger brother, William, a businessman who greatly admired him. Beginning in the 1940s, Moreno's productivity was greatly enhanced by the ability and devotion of his second wife, Zerka. Over the next 20 years, J. L. and Zerka Moreno published several journals and wrote a number of books and articles. They embarked on an almost continuous schedule of lecture-demonstrations, training workshops, consultations, and speaking engagements in the United States and other countries. In addition, they worked together with patients at his sanitarium until the early 1960s. Students were also trained at the facility through the early 1970s.

At the age of 85, after a series of small strokes, Jacob L. Moreno died at his home in Beacon, New York, on May 14, 1974. He had chosen to stop eating in the weeks before his passing and gradually declined. During that time he welcomed old friends and visitors with openness and warmth (Sacks, 1977; Yablonsky, 1975). Moreno's epitaph was chosen by him in advance: "Here lies the man who brought laughter back into psychiatry."

Moreno said to his wife, Zerka, that he had created the system, and now it was up to her and the others to carry on the work. Psychodrama has expanded its range of activities significantly in the past decade, and these developments deserve further comment. The primary exponent of Moreno's work has been Zerka, and the following section will briefly introduce some significant aspects of her life.

ZERKA TOEMAN MORENO: A BIOGRAPHICAL SKETCH

Zerka Toeman, the youngest of four children, was born in 1917 to a Jewish family living in Amsterdam, The Netherlands. In 1931 they moved to England, and Zerka attended a high school and college in Willesden Green, a suburb of London. An older sister in her early twenties became psychotic and was diagnosed as having a form of schizophrenia. This event and her sister's continuing illness were later to prove instrumental in Zerka's meeting Moreno. In addition there was an important transpersonal element to the bond that occurred between Zerka and J. L. Zerka was sensitive and receptive to voices that spoke from her inner, wiser self. For instance, when Zerka was 18 and living in England in 1935, a year before her sister's psychotic break, a voice told her to go to America. She didn't act on it then; in fact, she moved back to the Netherlands alone, to work as a governess. Four years later, Zerka was walking in an elegant suburb on a quiet night, and again she had the impelling feeling that she had to go to America. The sense of a presence spoke to her: "Yes, you must go! There is something important—someone waiting for you." This time she did emigrate to New York and settled there.

In 1941, with great danger threatening her older sister and her sister's family in Belgium, Zerka was able to negotiate the visas allowing them to emigrate to America. When they arrived, her sister had relapsed into schizophrenia. Dr. Emil Gutheil referred them to Moreno's sanitarium. During the treatment of Zerka's sister, Moreno experienced a powerful sense of "tele" with Zerka, as if he "recognized" her. Likewise, he and the idea of psychodrama fascinated her.

Because of her background in the theater, fine arts, and psychology, Zerka became involved with psychodrama and worked as a trained auxiliary in the care of her sister as well as other patients at Moreno's sanitarium. Her interest in Moreno and his work continued to grow as she began to share administrative and secretarial responsibilities of his diverse and complex enterprise. It became clear to her that Moreno was the "someone waiting for you," and in 1949 they were married. Jonathan, their only child, was born in 1952.

"In many ways we are all survivors." Zerka has taught this concept in a number of workshops. It is an insight that came to her during a grueling personal experience. In 1957, Zerka was diagnosed as having cancer (chondrosarcoma) in the bone of her right shoulder. This involved the amputation of her entire right arm just in time to save her life. Her handicap did not deter her from continuing to serve as Moreno's "right hand" (as she laughingly phrased it). Following his death in 1974, she carried on with teaching and writing about psychodrama, group dynamics, and sociometry. She remains the foremost exponent of the method in the world today, traveling internationally, holding workshops, and teaching at major conferences. She is currently working on Moreno's extensive autobiography, begun before his death, with the help of their son. Jonathan Moreno is a professor of philosophy and bioethics, as well as being active in the field of psychodrama.

OTHER PIONEERS IN PSYCHODRAMA AND SOCIOMETRY

During the 1940s and 1950s a number of professionals worked with Moreno in practicing and developing psychodrama, sociodrama, and sociometry in psychiatry, sociology, criminology, education, and other fields (Z. Moreno, 1966). Some of the more prominent figures included the following:

Max and Sylvia Ackerman   Doris Twitchell Allen
Didier Anzieu   Robert Boguslaw
Edgar Borgatta   Eya Fechin Branham
Anna and Nah Brind   Anthony Brunse
J. A. Bustamante   E. A. Carp
Gertrude Harrow-Clemens   Raymond J. Corsini
Robert Drews   Dean Elefthery
Eugene Eliasoph   James Enneis
Ernest Fantel   Leon J. Fine
Abel K. Fink   Robert Bartlett Haas
Margaret Hagan   Martin Haskell

Frances Herriott
Richard Korn
Serge Lebovici
Gretel Leutz
Joseph Mann
Donnell Miller
Walter E. O'Connell
Frisso Potts
Anne Ancelin Schutzenberger
Nahum Shoobs
Adaline Starr
Helga Straub
E. Paul Torrance
Daniel Widlocher

Abraham Knepler
Helen Hall Jennings
Gerald W. Lawlor
Rosemary Lippitt
Joseph I. Meiers
Neville Murray
Abel Ossorio
James M. Sacks
Barbara Seabourne
Bruno Solby
Berthold Stovkis
Israel E. Sturm
Hannah B. Weiner
Lewis Yablonsky

FURTHER DEVELOPMENTS IN PSYCHODRAMA

Following Moreno's passing, the field shifted from the domination of its founder to a more democratic and decentralized distribution of authority. The American Society for Group Psychotherapy and Psychodrama (ASGPP),[1] the organization Moreno founded in 1942, became the general organizing force, and it has embarked on a path toward more professionalization. In this spirit, the American Board of Examiners in Psychodrama, Sociometry, and Group Psychotherapy[2] was established in 1975 as a body with the authority and responsibility to test and certify trainers and practitioners. The highest level of certification is indicated by the initials T.E.P., which stand for trainer, educator, and practitioner. This appellation refers to a director who is recognized as being able to train other directors. A list of certified trainers and practitioners can be obtained by writing to the American Board.

In 1976, the Federation of Trainers and Training Programs in Psychodrama (FTTPP) was organized to standardize the curriculum in the various institutes. One of its several contributions was the idea of a "tabella," a registered record of training that a student takes to educational sessions led by TEPs and into which training hours are entered. Information regarding training can be obtained through the American Board office.

The ASGPP continues to serve as the major organization for people interested in psychodrama and more innovative approaches to individual, family, and group psychotherapy. It edits the *Journal of Group Psychotherapy, Psychodrama, and Sociometry* and holds annual meetings that offer useful experiential workshops. A number of regional divisions and meetings have also been organized. (Joining and using the ASGPP as a vehicle for networking and sharing professional experiences is an excellent way to meet fellow professionals, who comprise a particularly spontaneous and interesting group.)

Psychodrama is well established and well integrated with the mainstream of psychiatry in other countries, especially Brazil, Argentina, Sweden, and Germany. There are also major connections between psychodrama and group psychotherapy in France, Australia, Italy, Spain, Mexico, Japan, and Greece. In the United States, psychodrama is used in many psychiatric settings, often by professionals who are not formally certified or affiliated with the ASGPP. It is hoped that these people can be encouraged to join with their colleagues in the continuing development of the field.

Training at Beacon, New York, continued until around 1980 under the supervision of Zerka Moreno and various visiting directors. After this, it was kept active by the Horsham Clinic until the center was closed in 1984. The property was sold, and the original psychodrama stage has been moved to the Jonathan Steiner Hall at Boughton Place in Highland, New York.

There is no question that by the end of the 1970s many of Moreno's ideas and methods had been assimilated into the mainstream of psychotherapy and to a significant extent into education, management, and various types of training. Role playing, for example, is used in many settings, and yet its derivation from psychodrama is often unrecognized. As psychoanalysis is generally becoming less dominant in American psychiatry, a number of eclectic approaches are replacing its hegemony. Many of these methods can be traced, at least in part, to Moreno's contributions.

The field of drama therapy[3] is an interesting example. Before 1965 it was primarily an activity involved with helping psychiatric patients to rehearse and present skits and plays that were emotionally relevant. Since then, however, the idea of integrating spontaneity and activities like theater games has brought this field closer to Moreno's ideal. Many drama therapy programs include psychodrama in their curricula. They have developed a number of techniques that would be useful in psychodrama as warm-ups, for the promotion of group dynamics, and as methods for catalyzing creative processes (Johnson, 1984).

Creative drama in the schools in England and the United States has also been a growing field. The emphasis on spontaneous improvisations is certainly in the spirit of Moreno's ideals, although it arose independently through the work of Winifred Ward (around 1925, in Illinois) and several English dramatists and teachers, such as Peter Slade and Dorothy Heathcote (in the 1940s).

There has also been a growing convergence of the creative and expressive therapies, including psychodrama, art, music, dance, movement, poetry, crafts, puppetry, and drama. All of these share some similar goals, namely, the liberation and use of spontaneity as part of the healing process.

More important, the field of psychodrama is expanding beyond the boundaries of therapy to include a variety of artistic, recreational, and educational applications such as Jonathan Fox's Playback Theater in Poughkeepsie, New York (Fox, 1981) and Rosalie Minkin's educational psychodramatic theater for teenagers and the aged in Philadelphia. Programs in creativity training for professionals and many other innovative applications are being developed by other workers in the field. These all reflect the dynamic potentials of psychodrama and sociodrama.

The words of Carl G. Jung (1948) are relevant in thinking about the evolution of psychodrama before and after Moreno's death:

> The pioneer in a new field has the good fortune to be able to draw valid conclusions from his total experience. The efforts and exertions, the doubts and uncertainties of this voyage of discovery have penetrated his marrow too deeply to allow the perspective and clarity which are necessary for a comprehensive presentation. Those of the second generation, who base their work on his groping attempts, the chance hits, the circuitous approaches, the half-truths and mistakes of the pioneer, are less burdened and can take more direct roads, envisage further goals. They are able to cast off many doubts and hesitations, concentrate on essentials, and in this way, map out a simpler and clearer picture of the newly discovered territory. The simplification and clarification redound to the benefit of those of the third generation who are thus equipped from the onset with an over-all chart. With this chart they are enabled to formulate new problems and mark out the boundaries more sharply than ever before. (p. xi)

We have entered the second and third generations of explorations in the field of psychodrama, as well as in the related methods that seek to utilize the creative potential in the human psyche.

In Moreno's case, his vitality and enthusiasm were easily channeled into the active leadership role that is necessary when using psychodramatic methods. His own style tended toward the narcissistic and grandiose, although he could also be highly intuitive, warm, and inclusive. Zerka and other directors over the years, members of the second and third generations, have demonstrated that it is possible to use these approaches with more refinement and gentleness than the originator himself did. Even though Moreno's exuberance was an essential asset that gave him the courage to promote his ideas in an inhospitable professional climate, his personal style added to the difficulties in gaining acceptance for his work. The difficulties psychodrama encountered in being recognized and some speculations about the reasons for these resistances will be discussed in Chapter 4.

REFERENCES

Chace, Marian. (1945). Rhythm in movement as used in St. Elizabeth's Hospital. In J. L. Moreno (Ed.), *Group Psychotherapy: A Symposium* (pp. 243–245). Beacon, NY: Beacon House.

Fox, Jonathan. (1981). Playback Theater: The community sees itself. In Gertrud Schattner & Richard Courtney (Eds.), *Drama in Therapy* (Vol. 2) (pp. 295–308). New York: Drama Book Specialists.

Johnson, David Read. (1984). The field of drama therapy. *Journal of Mental Imagery, 7*(1), 105–109.

Jung, Carl G. (1948). Foreword. In Esther G. Harding, *Psychic energy: Its source and its transformation* (p. xi). New York: Pantheon Books.

Moreno, Zerka T. (1966). Evolution and dynamics of the Group Psychotherapy Movement. In J. L. Moreno et al. (Eds.), *The international handbook of group psychotherapy* (pp. 27–128). New York: Philosophical Library.

Sacks, James M. (1977). Reminiscence of J. L. Moreno. *Group, 1*(3), 194–200.

Yablonsky, Lewis. (1975). Psychodrama lives. *Human Behavior, 4*(2), 25–29.

[1] American Society for Group Psychotherapy and Psychodrama, 116 East 27th Street (11th Floor), New York, NY 10016. Phone: (212) 725–0033.

The ASGPP holds an annual convention and several regional meetings, as well as sponsoring a professional journal. You may write to them regarding membership information, upcoming meetings, and other matters.

[2] The American Board of Examiners in Psychodrama, Sociometry, and Group Psychotherapy, P.O. Box 15572, Washington, DC 20003–0572. Phone: (202) 965–4115.

You may write to the American Board of Examiners and ask for a list of certified trainers or practitioners of psychodrama in your area. They will also supply information regarding the requirements for certification.

[3] The National Association for Drama Therapy, 19 Edwards Street, New Haven, CT 06511. Phone: (203) 624–2146. The N.A.D.T. is another organization which is integrating concepts of spontaneity and dramatic work. You may write them regarding graduate programs in drama therapy.

4

Resistances to Psychodrama

The work of J. L. Moreno has great potential but has not been widely accepted in the United States. In fact, Moreno was considered somewhat of a maverick by the majority of professionals in psychiatry and psychology. In spite of this, many of Moreno's methods have been incorporated into the new forms of psychotherapy developed in the last several decades. Because he was a significant contributor to the evolution of psychotherapy, it is important to recognize and redeem the best of Moreno's insights as sources of continuing inspiration. There are two general groups of reasons for the neglect of his ideas: Historically, Moreno's concepts were far in advance of their time, and personally, Moreno behaved in ways that alienated a large number of his fellow professionals.

THE HISTORICAL CONTEXT

Resistance to the concept of psychodrama was based on the following factors:

1. Psychodrama as a mode of therapy was radically different from the approaches of both the analytic and nonanalytic schools of psychotherapy that were considered acceptable practice during the period between 1935 and 1955.

2. When at last the field of psychotherapy began to open up to various innovations, the competing forms that integrated psychoanalytic concepts with some of Moreno's ideas, such as group psychotherapy, family therapy, humanistic psychology, Transactional Analysis, and Gestalt therapy, received most of the attention. Psychodrama remained relatively isolated because it tended to be practiced in the classical form.

3. In academic psychology, behaviorism in the 1950s and 1960s was evolving therapeutic methods that served to give psychologists a distinct identity and tradition of their own. Interestingly, activities such as directed imagination, modeling, and behavioral practice shared commonalities with the principles of psychodrama, but the connection was rarely made in the literature or teaching.

4. Moreno's practice of repeatedly contrasting himself with the dominant school of psychoanalysis clearly defied the intellectual trends of the period. Throughout the 1940s, psychoanalysis had a large number of well-educated, respected proponents, and it offered a relatively comprehensive and intellectually rich, dynamic theoretical system. Its method was interesting, novel, and popular among a successful portion of society, many of whom were influential by their proximity to the world of media (i.e., novels, magazines, movies). The orthodox Freudian approach itself was being modified in exciting ways during this period, as in the work of the "neoanalytic" schools of thought of Karen Horney, Harry Stack Sullivan, and Erick Fromm. In contrast, Moreno worked outside this system, almost alone, with a small and shifting number of students.

Psychoanalysis during the 1940s was itself the avant garde movement to most young psychiatrists. Its aura of authority was enhanced by the many European psychoanalysts who had emigrated to escape Hitler's anti-Semitic pogroms. Thus, this school of thought also attracted the sympathy of the majority. In this climate, although Moreno's criticisms of analytic method had some validity, there was clearly little interest by people who were newly discovering it. (Psychoanalysis began to emerge as the caricature of orthodoxy only at the end of the 1950s, partly because many of its major proponents became unwilling to assimilate the new approaches available in psychotherapy.)

Although Moreno acknowledged Freud as an original and important thinker, he made few attempts to integrate his approach with the psychoanalytic theory. (One of the goals of this book is to help bridge the two theories.) However, in some countries, such as France and Argentina, psychodramatic and psychoanalytic ideas have been successfully synthesized since the mid-1950s.

5. Private practice was the economic context chosen by professionals with the highest status. Analytic approaches were more suited to the kinds of problems addressed in such settings. In contrast, Moreno's early work with prisoners, the retarded, and psychotics made his "data base" seemingly less relevant or applicable to the concerns of the majority of professionals. Since the 1960s, however, there has emerged a large body of work that clearly demonstrates that psychodrama can be highly effective in dealing with standard "neurotic" problems.

6. The time required for doing psychodrama was another factor that made it less practical for use in clinical practice. A classical psychodramatic session generally requires at least 2 or 3 hours to develop an adequate warm-up, action, and processing. Although the method can generate as much material in one session as it might take many ordinary verbal sessions to access, it was not compatible with the tradition of the "50-minute hour." Most mainstream therapists considered it impractical and economically unfeasible. To further complicate the considerations of its use, classical psychodramatic therapy stirred up so much emotion that it also required more aftercare and people available for support.

7. Directive approaches, involving advice, exhortation, and inspirational lectures, had become unfashionable by the mid-1930s; they were associated with authoritarian behaviors practiced by people raised before the turn of the century. Cultural tastes were shifting away from family-centered, patriarchal educational and religious traditions. Refreshing alternatives were found in the nondirective, nonjudgmental approaches, such as psychoanalysis or Carl Rogers' nondirective therapy. Although psychodrama follows

the needs of the patient and is client-centered in its essence, it is also active and directive. Unfortunately, these aspects associated it with an outmoded advice-giving style.

8. Activity itself, in the therapeutic context, was also considered unfashionable. The patients commonly described in the early professional literature had hysterical or compulsive behaviors, and one of the goals of therapy was controlling their "acting out." In fact, psychodrama may be used successfully to help people be less pathologically expressive; however, at that time it was mistakenly suspected of fostering a kind of excessive catharsis that might reinforce pathological patterns (Murray, 1976).

The activity required by the therapist also tended to disqualify psychodrama. One of the main principles in psychoanalytic practice stressed the importance of evoking a transference by means of the therapist's playing a neutral role, and any behavior that disclosed the therapist's personality was considered an unacceptable contamination of this process. Part of psychoanalytic training involved the discipline of the therapist's learning to control overt activity, which was considered a form of countertransference arising out of a "neurotic need to be helpful." Thus, any therapist who advocated active approaches was degraded professionally because the behavior was interpreted as rationalizing personal needs. Interestingly, the 1920s through the 1940s were also the decades that promoted the (now absurd) notion that "spoiling" children arose from the habit of picking up or feeding babies when they cried. A rigidly abstinent model was in vogue, both in child rearing and in the psychotherapeutic community. Action approaches were not differentiated from acting out and were slandered for promoting neurosis. The prejudice against being active in therapy has continued even to the present in some quarters.

9. Some elements of the theater have a long history of being distrusted. During the first half of this century, the theater contained aspects that were inauthentic, histrionic, sexualized, and in other ways disreputable. Moreno worked to rehabilitate this ancient art form and to restore its accessibility to everyone. He developed the practice of spontaneity as opposed to highly structured and rehearsed performances. Theoretically and practically, he created an alternative to the spiritless theater of his time. However, his terminology in psychodrama, taken from the theater, associated it with the very thing he was hoping to change (Blatner, 1968). For example, the term "role playing" has often been used as a reference to fraudulent behavior, but Moreno used the term to designate

a process that served to increase authenticity (J. Moreno, 1975).

10. Through the years, psychodrama stimulated some people without proper training who called their activities by that name. Unfortunately, they often misunderstood fundamental principles, and sometimes their work was the opposite of Moreno's ideals. For example, these directors would fail to warm up their groups effectively, and the protagonist was constrained to suffer in irrelevant and contrived situations. Another abuse of the method occurred when it became a vehicle for harsh confrontation. Following exposure to a brief demonstration or a weekend workshop, misguided people would attempt to conduct sessions, and the results could be destructive. Instead of criticizing the directors for their inadequate training, more often the method was blamed.

11. Group approaches were unfashionable in the early years of psychotherapy. The process of releasing an individual's repression had only recently begun; it was a major challenge for people to admit to themselves that they harbored socially unacceptable feelings, sexual thoughts, or aggressive fantasies. It was even more difficult in a one-to-one session with a nonjudgmental therapist. To speak of or show such feelings in a group with other people was almost unthinkable. In this context it is easy to understand why privacy and confidentiality were a major attraction and the hallmark of psychotherapy. In the early years, Moreno's advocacy of group psychotherapy was out of step with the mainstream (Bromberg, 1957). As people in our culture became more familiar with the universality of emotions and thoughts, the fear of working in a group lessened. Indeed, learning that one's feelings were shared by others became a major factor for healing in group therapy. Even today, people are instinctively wary of action methods because the conventional defense systems of verbal interchange are superseded.

12. A related issue was that therapists were for the most part introverted, having been trained in an academic model of the passive student role. There was little social or professional preparation for coping with groups. Shyness was so prevalent that it was not considered suboptimal functioning. Therefore, group approaches were sensed as threatening to the therapist, and this fear was unconsciously projected onto patients with the rationalization that "they" would find it unacceptable. As group work became a recognized therapeutic approach, this excuse was no longer acceptable.

13. Psychodrama, as it was presented originally, in what I term its classical form, was quite difficult to learn and apply. The training could be gotten only from Moreno, and often this involved traveling

to upstate New York and living at his institute–sanitarium. Since most other approaches could be learned in local academic centers, only people who really had the initiative and drive to learn about his alternative method of treatment exerted the effort to seek him out. Thus, the small number of trained students limited the impact and promotion of psychodrama in the field of psychotherapy.

14. By the early part of this century, religion and philosophy were domains that had been separated from science. The distinct fields were kept apart with great emotional conviction. Moreno's active inclusion of philosophical and religious themes in his writings and personal presentations again went against the norm. His idiosyncratic philosophy challenged the established religious traditions. Moreover, the emerging field of psychiatry was trying very hard to gain recognition from the larger scientific community. It tried to accomplish this by uniting itself with the evolution of medicine, which was adhering to scientific methods. Moreno's inclusion in the psychiatric mainstream was severely thwarted by his writings and behaviors, which tended to be inspirational and poetic rather than helping to build a body of data on the science of the mind.

PERSONAL FACTORS

The preceding historical context is incomplete without also including the personal dimension, because it helps form an inextricable matrix. It has been said that Moreno was a genius, and this is probably accurate. A genius tends to be inconsistent with the models we hold of how people should be or what to expect from them. Moreno presented himself and promoted his method in ways that at times could be considered inappropriate.

His faults do not diminish the value of his concepts. People who choose, as he did, to live out their lives in a public setting are bound to reveal their limitations. Visionaries naturally find their lives in the spotlight. For us to fixate on the weaknesses that become so obvious in that context is trivial; it betrays our own envy and reveals the poverty of our own vision. The challenge is simple and clear: What can we build based on the material such visionaries have had the courage to put forth?

The personal factors that contributed to resistance to Moreno's philosophy include the following:

1. Moreno's use of the open group session was shocking to the

mainstream of the profession. Since his earliest work involved "mass therapy" through the use of impromptu theater, he was convinced of the potential of psychodrama applied in large group settings. He was familiar and comfortable with such contexts. In the 1940s he opened a studio on the Upper East Side of New York City, where he worked with 30 to 100 or more people who attended on a weekend evening and paid a price equivalent to that of a movie. The audience became the source of the protagonists in the psychodramas and sometimes served as the auxiliaries.

Professionals were concerned that the people who became participants in the psychodramas and experienced powerful emotions did not have enough time for fully processing their feelings. Furthermore, there appeared to be no precaution taken regarding whether the protagonists had supportive social networks available to help them after the sessions. Apparently there were no casualties from this practice; nonetheless, the disregard of confidentiality and lack of follow-up seemed unprofessional. Use of the open session continues to be controversial among psychodramatists even today.

On the other hand, Moreno consciously chose this practice as a vehicle for promoting his ideas and methods, which he felt transcended the conventional requirements of therapy. The open sessions attracted many professionals, usually out of curiosity. Often, like Fritz Perls, they picked up some techniques and then moved on. Others were fascinated enough by what they experienced to become students, and some became teachers of Moreno's concepts and techniques.

2. Partly based on his philosophy of doing therapy with a society as well as individuals, Moreno made a decision to accept students from other professions, and laypersons as well. In this, his orientation was similar to Freud's regarding the importance of lay analysis (Bettelheim, 1983). Moreno knew that psychodrama, sociometry, group dynamics, and the other aspects of his system had as much, if not more, application in fields beyond the therapeutic model—education, sociology, religion, the theater, community action, and so forth. His students came from these and many other areas of interest. Once again, however, this practice diluted the professionalism of his work to some who were influential in the mainstream of académe and psychiatry.

3. The dissemination of psychodramatic methods and ideas was significantly inhibited by the lack of available written material. The only books about psychodrama (until the mid-1960s) were by Moreno himself, and these were not well written. Furthermore,

although there was a valid need for new terms to describe phenomena that had no other equivalents, creating unfamiliar terms
increased the difficulty of learning his system. Professionals
encountered another impediment in Moreno's failure to build
bridges to other psychological theories. (Actually, some of
Moreno's ideas have much in common with certain concepts of
Otto Rank and Alfred Adler, among others.) Students found little
practical how-to-do-it guidance in his introductory texts. Unfortunately, Moreno's style of writing was often redundant, diffuse,
rambling, turgid, and suffused with philosophical speculations and
personal-historical reminiscences.

In this regard, the reading of his major texts was further complicated by the inclusion of "political" issues. Moreno would inter-
sperse assertions about the priority of his contributions and dispute
the originality of such leaders in the field as S. R. Slavson or Kurt
Lewin. There is a place for this type of editorializing, but it is not
in articles or books purportedly covering matter-of-fact material.
This competitive stance with other professionals and with psychoanalysis in general distracted the reader into a demand for a shift of
loyalty, which was too much to expect. Even if many of his argu-
ments were valid, their inappropriate placement amid the technical
material and his querulous tone discouraged the development of a
serious, professional audience.

4. Although Moreno's theories contain some powerfully innovative ideas, his system is insufficiently coherent or clear. If examined with great care, it does possess an internally consistent and
genuinely holistic network of concepts, but such study demands
extraordinary devotion. Furthermore, I think the ideas require
refinement and some revision. Moreno made no effort to compare
his ideas with others in psychiatry or psychology, although this
might have made it easier for the reader to understand them.

5. Professional journals are major vehicles for the communication of new ideas, and Moreno's decision to edit and publish his
own journals had mixed results. His publicity and distribution
capability were obviously limited. Perhaps this system was the easi-
est way to guarantee that his ideas were published. The choice of
articles that did appear was too often lacking in rigor, which
diminished the general credibility of the journals themselves. From
the late 1930s through the early 1950s his publications, (i.e., *Sociometry, Group Psychotherapy,* and others) were vehicles for occasional articles by early innovators in psychotherapy and social psychology, such as Rudolf Dreikurs, Marian Chace, Nathan

Ackerman (who later became a pioneer in family therapy), Ronald Lippitt (who was one of the originators of the T-group), and others; nevertheless, they failed to project a professional image (Treadwell & Treadwell, 1972).

By the late 1950s, partly due to the emergence of alternative journals, Moreno's publications lost many of their eminent contributors and became instruments of his more specialized interests. Thus, he frequently published anecdotal reports, abstracts of presentations at the annual meetings of the ASGPP, and students' papers, and he advertised his training programs a little too obviously.

6. Moreno's personal style of presentation was another source of professional resistance. He was charismatic: dynamic, engaging, flamboyant, and dramatic. These qualities could also tend toward grandiosity and megalomania at times. As a director, he could be acutely perceptive of the dynamics in a psychodrama and yet might be insensitive to the needs of his audience. His essential vitality was refreshing to those who had become dissatisfied with the emotional constriction of the typical psychiatric presentation; however, the content of his talks, like his writings, could at times ramble into issues of personal history. His speaking would attract many people because his enthusiasm was contagious and the ideas were exciting. However, equal numbers would be offended because his manner of presentation tended to appear unprofessional and at times was simply boring, irrelevant, or "off-the-wall."

In some ways, I think Moreno consciously created his public image in an effort to embody and model his belief in spontaneity. However, to critique his behavior using his own definition— spontaneity is an adequate response to a new situation—I suggest that he was at times indulging in what he and others would have called pathological spontaneity. For example, when he talked about the creative force of the "Godhead" or the cosmic "Father," he was trying to convey his concept that everyone was a channel for this force, but it usually appeared that he overidentified with the role (Power, 1975).

7. In his relationships with associates and students, Moreno could be remarkably intuitive, creative, and inclusive. In running psychodrama sessions, these qualities communicated the aura of a true healer. At other times, he could be petty, insensitive, arrogant, capricious, overly controlling, and fairly narcissistic. As a result, he influenced many but kept few close friends.

Usually, people came into training, learned what they needed, and moved on. Even those who were loyal to him kept some degree of distance while they continued their own work. Moreno collaborated with several major figures in the field of psychiatry, but generally their experiences contained so many difficulties that they were not repeated. With students, Moreno could be friendly one moment and easily offended the next. It was easy to feel a genuine affection for him; however, with experience one learned to stay somewhat wary.

8. Organizationally, Moreno's efforts to maintain control of his ideas were counterproductive. He did not publicize the addresses of other directors in his journal, and the professionals who worked with him and later became alienated had no way of "networking" with others who shared their interest in his methods.

One of Moreno's motivations for dominating the training and propagation of his ideas was that he feared his methods would be used as separate elements apart from the unifying philosophy of spontaneity and the goal of healing the society. Sadly his fears were realized. Sociometry was applied in sociology without the commitment to helping the groups tested to utilize the information (Mendelson, 1977). Psychodrama was reported in many textbooks with no mention of the relation to its philosophical basis. Role playing has become a commonly used method in education and business, and yet most of its practitioners do not even know that it was originated by Moreno.

In attempting to personally control the evolution of psychodrama, Moreno inevitably spread himself too thin. He sometimes led others to expect support that he would not or could not deliver. His follow-up, an essential organizational skill, was often lacking. In turn, these interpersonal mishaps resulted in potential co-workers feeling snubbed or let down and ultimately thwarted the success of his endeavors and goals.

In summary, after considering the many difficulties involved, it is a tribute to Moreno's strengths of courage, persistence, and vision that his approach has survived as well as it has. A great deal of credit must go to his wife, Zerka, who moderated many of his faults and championed his work, both before and after his death. Without her it is doubtful he would have been as productive as he was or to what extent his ideas would have survived after their creator was gone. Anyone wishing to do more scholarly research on the history of Moreno or his ideas is directed to the medical library at Harvard University, which is the repository for the entire Moreno archives.

The major reason Moreno's ideas continue to stimulate professionals in a number of fields is that they are basically valid, powerful, and relevant, now more than ever. In a time of pervasive dehumanization, his contributions to developing the value and individuality of each person through sociometric and spontaneity-training principles are most timely. Many of Moreno's methods already have been put to use in encounter groups, sensitivity training, education, family therapy (Virginia Satir's technique of family sculpture is derived from the technique of the action sociogram), business, theater, the creative arts therapies, and many other innovations in psychotherapy.

For a system to be accepted, however, it is not enough for it to contain excellent ideas and powerful techniques. It must also be established as theoretically clear and coherent, professionally reputable, and scientifically effective. Otherwise, it will seem to be just a "gimmick." Because of the factors of historical unreadiness and Moreno's personal idiosyncrasies, his approach has not yet achieved the popular or professional recognition I think it deserves. This book is an effort to help remedy some of the confusion and to present Moreno's concepts in a more accessible format.

REFERENCES

Bettelheim, Bruno. (1983). *Freud and man's soul.* New York: Alfred A. Knopf.

Blatner, H. A. (1968). Comments on some commonly-held reservations about psychodrama. *Group Psychotherapy, 21*(1), 20–25.

Bromberg, Walter. (1957). Evolution of group psychotherapy. *Group Psychotherapy, 10*(2), 111–113.

Mendelson, Peter D. (1977). Sociometry as a life philosophy. *Group Psychotherapy, Psychodrama, and Sociometry, 30*, 70–85.

Moreno, Jonathan. (1975). Notes on the concept of role playing. *Group Psychotherapy, 28*, 105–107.

Murray, Neville. (1976). Psychodrama—post Moreno. In Arlene R. Wolberg, Lewis R. Wolberg, & Marvin L. Aronson (Eds.), *Group Psychotherapy* (pp. 16-20). New York: Stratton Intercontinental Book Corp.

Power, Joseph P. (1975). Moreno and the God controversy. *Group Psychotherapy, 28*, 164–167.

Treadwell, Thomas, & Treadwell, Jean. (1972). The pioneer of the group encounter movement. *Group Psychotherapy and Psychodrama, 25*, 16–26.

PART II
Philosophical Foundations

5

Philosophical Foundations of Psychodrama: Co-creativity and Responsibility

In this section, Moreno's theories will be extended by exploring some of his most important themes in greater depth. The most pervasive one is the place of creativity and the importance of cultivating this source of vitality in the processes of healing and growth. He felt that lack of creativity was one of the central problems in modern culture, contributing to both personal and social psychopathology.

Whereas the repression of sexual and aggressive impulses manifesting as neurosis was the primary focus of the psychoanalytic system during the first half of this century, the second half has revealed a different predominant problem—the retreat from responsibility. Associated pathology includes pervasive addictive behavior, anomie, values diffusion, and general stress disorders allied to a sense of personal helplessness.

The issue of responsibility was an important one in the works of Alfred Adler, Otto Rank, and Roberto Assagioli (Assagioli, 1974; Rank, 1945). In the last few decades, several therapies have arisen that specifically address this problem, including among others Assagioli's psychosynthesis, William Glasser's reality therapy, and Werner Erhard's est. Moreno's approach focuses on developing spontaneity, which strengthens a person's flexibility of mind for taking responsibility. Furthermore, specific skills can be practiced that convert a healthy willingness to explore possibilities and take initiative into confidence. From this point people can explore expanding their role repertoire, and through that process they experience themselves as being the locus of effective action. A wider role repertoire can offer choices about possible response strategies available. The ability to respond flexibly involves having alternatives. These elements can be cultivated in activities that free up spontaneity. Moreno's system offers excellent methods for developing spontaneity and creativity; in addition, it provides a unifying philosophical approach (Moreno, 1946).

Psychodramatic methods can also be used simply to empower people—to remind them of their potential as creative beings. Modern psychotherapy tends to emphasize helping patients to become aware of the psychological blocks that interfere with adequate adjustment. However, it is also important to develop methods for helping patients (and, in a preventive sense, teaching all people) to access those natural sources of vitality that help to maintain morale and sustain courage while the other tasks of unlearning and relearning continue to unfold (Patterson, 1967).

Psychodramatic methods offer superior tools for addressing both of these therapeutic imperatives.

PSYCHODRAMA'S PHILOSOPHICAL COMMANDMENT

The basic theory of psychodrama is based on the phenomenon that each of us can create what happens in our minds, that experience is malleable. Committed to helping people put their progress into action in the real world, psychodrama works from a foundation that is intrinsically practical in its philosophy and psychology. It constantly focuses on the individual's experience. Each person brings forth a slightly different set of variables; and as the environment changes and evolves, those changes become the building blocks of a person's story. Psychodrama is more like a form than a system, and the form is more like dance. Its features are expressed by change, reinterpretation, and an interpenetration with other art forms and various kinds of activities.

The central theme of Moreno's work is the reintegration of spontaneity and creativity as highly valued dimensions of experience and behavior. This aspect of human—and even universal—process is as essential to effective and vital functioning as the challenge described by Freud of bringing the light of consciousness to the dimensions of everyday life. Freud showed us how repression and other mental mechanisms could block the psyche from its fullest expression, and Moreno added to this the ideas and methods that can liberate the creative aspects of both the individual and the society.

Considering many people's somewhat alienated situation in life, one of the important bases of psychodrama is its ability to mobilize the power of the group to heal one of its members, and thereby heal itself. Recognition of how profoundly social we intrinsically are has a number of psychological and moral implications. The first of these is what the philosopher Nicholas Berdyaev (1954) stated as the essential divine commandment: "To cultivate creativity in ourselves and others." Creativity has become an important theme in modern philosophy as our civilization begins to grasp the real implications of the concept of evolution—the inevitable process of growth and change.

Psychodramatic methods utilize a number of basic human capabilities in order to increase creativity. These include imagination, physical action, group dynamics, improvisation, and the opportunity to experiment in the special context of drama. The use of the innate power of these psychosocial resources in the form of an integrated method can facilitate growth in psychotherapy, education, and other fields.

THE LIBERATION OF SPONTANEITY

The capacity for responsibility is developed through the practice of a number of component abilities, such as initiative, improvisation, and a fearlessness to question conventional limitations or traditional modes of thought. Other elements of a flexible mind include curiosity, testing limits, exuberance, expressiveness, questioning, seeking attention, imaginativeness, intuitiveness, and the kind of freedom and social experimentation that occur in sociodramatic play. If these sound like the essential qualities of healthy, innocent young children, they are! Elements of spontaneity are our natural heritage, and they must be reclaimed and reintegrated if we are to utilize the tremendous psychological energies that can serve as resources for helping us to cope with the challenges of an increasingly changing world.

Ashley Montagu, a noted anthropologist and commentator on contemporary issues, wrote an important book *Growing Young* (1981). In it, he points out that there is a sociobiologic tendency in the human species to retain youthful qualities, and that this tendency, called "neoteny," has an adaptive advantage from an evolutionary standpoint. He writes: "Hence, the implications of all this should be fully understood and recognized: the importance of the sociodramatic experiences in the life of the child continue into the life of the adult" (p. 163).

Sociodramatic play refers to the kind of improvisatory, informal, make-believe, imaginative enactment that constitutes a goodly portion of the exploratory behavior of the young child. In our culture, this has been neglected or suppressed as children grow older; it is replaced by an emphasis on competitive games; rehearsed, performance-oriented drama; or other highly disciplined art forms.

Yet the phenomenon of free play is important and deserves both recognition and investigation as a natural way to learn, socialize, and explore and expand one's role repertoire in an environment oriented to healthy fun (Blatner & Blatner, 1987). The philosophy of psychodrama is based on the phenomenon of the universality of play in its many-faceted cultural expressions (Huizinga, 1955). As mentioned before, Moreno's theories and methods are rooted in his experiments with the play of children in the parks of Vienna in 1908.

Developing a technology for cultivating responsibility and creativity requires not only the establishment of a systematic approach but also a recognition that such an educational process must deal with a widespread personal and cultural layer of resistance. We are only now emerging from a social structure in which the behaviors that are part of spontaneity and creativity have been seen as negative qualities, too often treated with criticism or punishment. As people experiment with these behaviors again, there is a tendency to feel anxiety or guilt. Ideas that generate anxiety or socially negative consequences tend to get pushed out of people's conscious awareness. This process is accompanied by a variety of rationalizations and the establishment of norms that value more constricted, socially approved forms of behavior.

One major reason for this deflection of the spontaneous aspect of our minds is that it threatens the stability and authority of the hierarchical cultural systems. However, in a changing world, this stability is already shaken. The society's resource of creative minds is the very quality needed to design constructive new approaches. Our vast technological development has resulted in a major shift from a culture that simply passes along the knowledge of the elders; through a culture that generates new knowledge in the parental generation; and into a culture that actively utilizes the discoveries of younger people, as is happening with resources generated by the computer phenomenon. Margaret Mead (1970) called this a transition from a "prefigurative" through a "configurative" to a "postfigurative" culture.

IMAGINATION—OUR UNIQUE CAPACITY

Let us consider that what really differentiates humans from other animals is not so much our opposable thumb, erect posture, or even our ability to reason, but rather our imagination. This is the source of the richness of language, a process of metaphor built upon metaphor. Imagination is an elusive phenomenon, and we are only beginning to truly use it as a resource in our culture. Psychodrama evolved as a group of methods designed to capitalize on this dimension of mind, to focus and apply its potentialities.

Creativity relies on imagination to generate unique solutions, new combinations of existing elements, and new directions and possible outcomes. *The creative act first begins in a person's ability to be open to multiple internal and external messages and then to form a response that captures the spontaneity of the decision.* Imagination is a central component of spontaneity in many cases. For example, instead of directly willing some behavior, we can learn to imaginatively project our intention outside ourselves, picturing or sensing our goal. We imagine ourselves being "drawn" into the goal and then relinquishing some degree of self-conscious control of how we achieve it. (This I call "the receptive part of intentionality.") The process may be found in the martial arts of the East, some of their adaptations in Western athletics, applications of Ericksonian hypnosis, and a variety of recent practices in dance, creative writing, music, and art.

In psychodrama, the group's imagination is warmed up, and one person at a time becomes the focus of the group. The method involves an intentional movement into imagination, an opening into the place where the experience of spontaneity flows. From this comes creativity, a theme that has been written about a good deal in the last few decades. Although the various authors seem to agree that creativity is based on an integration of processes that are both conscious and unconscious, emotional and rational, intellectual and physical, they do not address themselves to how to cultivate the integrated process. Psychodrama and its associated approaches offer just such a method.

THE GROUP AS A LABORATORY

A basic principle of science is that deductive reasoning is not sufficient in really learning about life; experiments must be performed. There is a recognition that in complex situations there may be a number of variables that cannot be anticipated and are only discoverable in the actual trial of the hypothesis. In psychological issues, this may be the equivalent of saying that verbal discussion alone is an insufficient source of genuine learning. Thus, a more multidimensional approach is needed, allowing for the clarification of problems and the testing of new approaches. The most obvious and natural one to use is the arena in which children test out their experiences and abilities—the realm of make-believe play. In adulthood, this becomes the activity of drama.

The dramatic setting does not have to be oriented toward performance; it includes the familiar use of simulations, such as in the training of astronauts or pilots. Businesses that market-test a product, architects and inventors who build models and prototypes, all reflect the need to interface human factors and complex technological systems.

In psychology and interpersonal relations, issues can be equally complex. They too require exploration and practice in action, not simply discourse. There are factors such as getting the feel of a new behavior, desensitizing oneself to another's resistance, refining one's nonverbal style of communication, and obtaining encouragement, all of which come only through the more action-oriented, experiential modes of learning.

In psychodrama, participants engage in an informal type of science, one that provides a laboratory of relative safety and immediate feedback for trying out a variety of possible coping strategies in order to advance personal growth. In this sense, consider the following quotation from John A. Wheeler, an eminent physicist: "Science advances only by making all possible mistakes . . . . the main thing is to make the mistakes as fast as possible—and to recognize them" (Wheeler, 1981, p. 26).

Thus, consider again the common basis of drama, psychodrama, and the play of children. The real value and importance of children's play is becoming increasingly appreciated in the fields of child development, and the implications of this pervasive phenomenon include play's function as a catalyst for creativity (Brown & Gottfried, 1985). The psychodynamics and benefits of playfulness are discussed in the book *The Art of Play* (Blatner & Blatner, 1987).

Psychodrama demands a level of personal involvement and taking responsibility on the part of the participants that is fairly unique in psychotherapy. The obvious philosophical dimension of this principle is worth noting. Some of the modern trends in philosophy reflect a view of humanity that calls for a significant increase of responsibility; they include existentialism, humanism, new directions in theology, transcendentalism, creativity and process, and linguistic analysis. In addition to the developing technologies of the physical realm, we are also discovering technologies in the psychosocial sphere. Group dynamics, dream work, imagination training, biofeedback, cooperative games, spontaneity in athletics, body work, and many other methods from the human potential movement continue to catalyze a more personal and collective form of lifelong learning (Ferguson, 1980).

In summary, the common theme of a number of disciplines involves the challenge to take responsibility in our lives, to teach each other, to discover together, and to explore new possibilities. This is also the challenge of our age, since we are continually presented with changes and new events. Psychodramatic methods can effectively deal with many of the complexities of modern life. It is a method that, by virtue of its commitment to creativity, expects to change and evolve also. The methods are malleable tools that can be modified to be relevant to new technologies and new ideas. Taking responsibility and bringing creativity to the present moment are basic elements of psychodrama.

REFERENCES

Assagioli, Roberto. (1974). *The act of will.* New York: Penguin.

Berdyaev, Nicolai A. (1954). *The meaning of the creative act* (D. A. Lowrie, Trans.). New York: Harper & Bros. (Original work published in 1911.)

Blatner, Adam, & Blatner, Allee. (1987). *The art of play: An adult's guide to reclaiming imagination and spontaneity.* New York: Human Sciences Press.

Brown, Catherine Caldwell, & Gottfried, Allen W. (Eds.). (1985). *Play interactions: The role of toys and parental involvement in children's development.* Skillman, NJ: Johnson & Johnson Baby Products Company, Pediatric Round Table Series.

Ferguson, Marilyn. (1980). *The Aquarian conspiracy.* Los Angeles: J. P. Tarcher.

Huizinga, Johann. (1955). Humo ludens: *A study of the play element in culture.* Boston: Beacon Press.

Mead, Margaret. (1970). *Culture and commitment.* Garden City, NY: Natural History Press/Doubleday.

Montagu, Ashley. (1981). *Growing young.* New York: McGraw-Hill.

Moreno, J. L. (1946). *Psychodrama* (Vol. 1). Beacon, NY: Beacon House.

Patterson, C. H. (1967). Divergence and convergence in psychotherapy. *American Journal of Psychotherapy, 21*(1), 4–7.

Rank, Otto. (1945). *Will therapy.* New York: Alfred A. Knopf.

Wheeler, John A. (1981, August). Quoted in John P. Wiley, Jr. Phenomena, comment, and notes. *Smithsonian,* P. 26.

6

Philosophical Foundations of Psychodrama: Metaphysics and Sociatry

The phenomena of spontaneity and creativity involve metaphysical categories, that is, issues that involve the deeper properties of reality itself, apart from the particular concerns of human history and existence. Understanding the universality of evolutionary processes in astronomy, geology, biology, and history leads to a corresponding recognition of the pervasive role of creative and spontaneous processes throughout nature. In other words, this recognition can function as a bridge to thinking about philosophical or spiritual issues. Moreno's psychology, of which psychodrama is only one part, is really rooted in his philosophy of life. These ideas were in some ways radical, yet in truth they were part of an emerging world view that is becoming increasingly recognized as relevant for our modern era (Moreno, 1972).

A philosophical tradition I have found helpful in thinking about Moreno's ideas is the "process thought" of Alfred North Whitehead, who developed his concepts in the late 1920s (Jentz, 1985). Although I doubt that Moreno and Whitehead knew much, if anything, about each other's work, they share some important similarities in their visions (Blatner, 1985). The idea of creativity is central in both systems. For Whitehead, creativity is a basic process in the universe. He viewed fundamental phenomena as consisting of events rather than things. There is an element of experience in each event, and there is an act of creativity in each experience; this process pervades the universe. These concepts are similar to some of Moreno's ideas (Moreno, 1971).

Whitehead saw in this universal action of creative process something that is congruent with the essential nature of "mind," in the broadest sense of the term. A number of contemporary philosophers have come to the same conclusion (Hartshorne, 1984). Moreover, this process is aware of itself holistically and is somewhat like a living organism. The relationship of the events to the wholeness is more like that of a cell to a whole organism or a dream to a conscious mind than a hierarchical structuring such as a child to a parent or a subject to a king. Charles Hartshorne, the foremost exponent of Whitehead's thought, has termed this view "the World Soul," a metaphor derived from Plato's *Timaeus* (Hartshorne, 1983). Other philosophers who have shared some of these views include Leibniz, Spinoza, Bergson, Berdyaev, Charles S. Peirce, Tielhard de Chardin, and, more recently, Ken Wilber. Moreno is obviously a part of this philosophical tradition because of his emphasis on the innate creativity of every person and the potential of spontaneity in every moment.

A transpersonal dimension exists that expresses archetypal phenomena through all beings and is expressed by the creativity and individuation of the beings themselves. This concept is my own synthesis of the ideas of process thought and Moreno. In addition, I offer the following thoughts about the place of individuality in this philosophical theory: Individuality is a universal phenomenon; even the smallest particles are moving in such complex patterns that no two events are exactly the same. The source of individuality is thus a relationship between order and spontaneity. This pervasive feature of existence is meaningful. The individuality of each being allows for the enhancement of creativity within the structure of the whole.

In human terms, this means that each person's individuality offers a unique opportunity for the expression of original ideas in the world. To understand individuality, consider just four of many possible aspects of a person: temperament, interests, imagery, and historical background. There are so many different variables in each of these categories that they easily create unique combinations when blended among themselves, even more so when combined with other aspects. To put it directly, you are the only you that ever has been and ever will be, and that is important. It means that when you celebrate your uniqueness and offer it to the whole, you are contributing a vital element to the dynamic unfolding of reality. Furthermore, you are appropriately responding to fundamental principles in the universe. It also points to an ethical challenge to help bring out the individuality of others.

EVOLVING CONCEPTS OF GOD

Moreno dared to integrate philosophical concepts into discussions of psychology and sociology at a time when such metaphysical speculation generally went against the empirical scientific tradition. But times have changed, and increasing numbers of scientists are considering the philosophical implications of the discoveries of the last century (Wilber, 1984).

The concept of God in the writings of both Moreno and White-head transcended any particular religion. Moreno's version was a poetic metaphor of the primal Father principle that appealed to all existence to help in the creative process. God in this sense is not omnipotent but represents a unifying force that requires our active participation in order to create greater harmony. Nikos Kazantsakis (1960) refers to this relationship in his passionate, contemplative book, *The Saviors of God.*

Moreno's insight was that we must shift our concept of God from a "He" God through a "Thou" God to an "I" God (Kraus, 1984). From this view he encouraged us to recognize and become active in our roles as co-creators of the world. However, Moreno's wording and emphasis on "I am the Father" seemed to be an excessive and personal proclamation, even though he meant it to apply to everyone. He wanted everyone to speak it in the first person and claim the right and obligation to be a creator, a "genius" (his term), a manifestation of this cosmic Father principle. In this century the theme of our existential responsibility has also been expressed by a variety of other theologians and philosophers.

I would add another step: Developmentally, it is important to go through the "I" God stage to own our responsibility, but I think we must continue to a place of sharing and experiencing the relationship as a "We." In addition, it would be more appropriate to disclaim identity in favor of full participation. Rather than thinking of ourselves as being God, we could identify ourselves as being co-creative parts of a far greater dynamic wholeness—all of which, including ourselves, is God.

At this point, I need to clarify that Moreno should be considered more of a visionary than a systematic philosopher, more a poet than a theoretician. He wrote with inspired devotion about his vision of people recognizing the divine nature within themselves. He developed methods to help them experience an encounter with others and with aspects of themselves that would help the world move toward a more creative and consciously interrelated mode of existence.

ENCOUNTER AND SOCIAL RESPONSIBILITY

Moreno believed that it was possible to improve significantly our level of social competence. He knew that techniques such as role reversal and a familiarity with working things out using psychodramatic principles in a dynamic group context could integrate social "therapy" into everyday life, where it was most needed and useful. His commitment to these goals went far beyond applications in the medical model. He wrote about and spoke of the value of his methods and concepts being taught in schools and churches and applied in the home. Psychodramatic approaches in their broadest sense are simply tools for implementing a personally responsible and lovingly creative philosophy of life.

Moreno believed that collective responsibility could also be cultivated. In developing the method of sociometry in the mid–1930s, Moreno attempted to foster spontaneity in human relations by allowing groups to give each other feedback in a systematic fashion. Other leaders borrowed from Moreno's experiments, which were precursors to the encounter group, not only in spirit but also in terms of actual historical influence. Unfortunately, the encounter group, though fashionable in the late 1960s and early 1970s, did not develop a knowledge of skills for improving interpersonal relationships. Encounter groups declined in popularity in the late 1970s, I think, because they were insufficiently grounded in an educational, skill-building, theoretical framework. For example, the method invited psychologizing that could too easily mix subtle game playing with genuine mutuality, and it tended to substitute short-term experiences of pseudo-intimacy for the acquisition of interpersonal skills that could be used in a variety of settings. However, I think a renewed and more rigorously applied approach to the use of group methods might remedy many of the major pitfalls and limitations of the encounter group.

The need for a method of social therapy (Moreno called it sociatry) is relevant because many people still interact in an inauthentic fashion. It is common to use others a sources of approval, admiration, rescue, or fear or as objects for displacement, projection, exhibitionism, and the like. Instead of working things out in a creative, cooperative fashion, many people symbolically seek to be excused from responsibility, establish a one-up position, try to get revenge, manipulate help or gifts, or justify their position. Expectations remain hidden, disguised, and the use of generalities, excessive abstractions, indirectness, excuses, and other communicative mystifications operates to deflect any attempts to deal directly (and therefore with more vulnerability) with others. Even more resistances are marshaled when attempts are made to examine the nature of the interactive process itself.

One aspect of this problem is that people are afraid of direct and authentically expressed interpersonal conflict, in part because they are ignorant of methods for its resolution. They are afraid of finding out whether and how much they are disliked or disrespected. They do not believe they could change this state of affairs if they knew about it; they do not know how to find out how their faults might be remedied; nor do they know ways of correcting others' misperceptions and achieving a more positive outcome. Ironically, this leads to the kinds of avoidances and maneuvers that often create the very conditions that are feared. The defenses against being humiliated when rejected manifest as behaviors that lead to rejection. It is clear that more work is indicated for elucidating the dynamics of the interpersonal field and for developing methods of remedying the pervasive patterns of immaturity in our culture.

Finally, the theme of the ability of people to help each other runs through Moreno's writings and ties together the interpersonal and existential dimensions. "The dethronement of the therapist and the dilution of the overtones of his role allow clearer perception of the basic primary relationship factor" (Bromberg, 1959, p. 59). Using role reversal, sociometric techniques, and similar methods for promoting more authentic encounters, people can be helped to access creative resources they might not have known about previously. Such approaches have relevance not only to psychotherapy but also to helping the social maturation of modern culture.

A PHILOSOPHY OF ENCOUNTER

The philosophical foundation of psychodrama is enriched when one considers that the underlying concern is to foster co-creativity itself. We live in a realm where thoughts are not sufficient to make things come true (a property more true for the world of dreams). One of the advantages of this material plane of existence is that the adventure of creativity—its aesthetic value—is heightened because the creations require work, cooperation, sacrifice, clear thinking, and genuine encounter between seemingly separate sentient beings. In this collective challenge, we are all artists. Although Otto Rank modified psychoanalytic theory to promote creativity in patients and Moreno used drama as a vehicle for similar purposes, a further expansion must occur to include the reality that we are all co-creating this world. Working collectively is an artistic goal worthy of the individual creator who is idealized in our hyperindividualized culture. We learn to experience ourselves as co-creators by implementing our ideals, hopes, and visions in real life, with family, friends, co-workers, and others we meet only tangentially. Our vitality has a chance to grow from the spontaneity (rather than habit or repetition) that we access to renegotiate relationships and to generate new events (Blatner, 1985).

The personal world of subjective phenomena and dreams and the objective world of consensual reality are both addressed in psychodrama. It works in what Winnicott (1971) called "the transitional space" or what Pruyser (1983) called "the illusionistic world." My own term for this dimension in which mind clearly is inextricably interactive with matter is "the liminal field." I use this term to emphasize the potential for real people to manifest more completely the effective power of mental co-creativity. Liminality is generally considered a kind of metaphoric doorway of transformative process, and as such it is applied as a description of the nature of certain rites of passage or other events in which participants' identities change significantly (Evie Lotze, 1986, personal communication). I suggest this applies to the nature of psychodrama—the "surplus reality" of dramatic vehicles become agents of personal transformation and healing.

Furthermore, I propose the ontological validity of the liminal field because it represents the full continuum of "reality" by encompassing the range of human experience. Our most vital involvements include elements of both subjective and objective perception (Blatner & Blatner, 1987). Furthermore, the idea of objective reality, so prevalent as the basis of what most people consider the "truth," may itself be an illusion, an abstraction that expresses our wish for the security of absolutes.

Whether in the form of a psychodramatic stage or any other therapeutic vehicle (including the psychoanalyst's couch), the liminal field can be used to help a patient toward "re-experiencing the old unsettled conflict, but with a new ending, [which] is the secret of every penetrating therapeutic result" (Alexander, 1946, p. 338). In addition, the future can be envisioned and clarified, thus adding the teleological force of will to the therapeutic process. And, of course, both past and future are brought into the expanded present moment, giving a more holistic potential to this existential approach.

SOCIATRY: A METAMEDICAL MODEL

If we were to recognize fully our place of responsibility and interrelatedness with everyone and everything, it would lead to an almost overwhelming sense of vulnerability at the complexity of the challenge. Yet we can give ourselves the time to grow (historically, cultural advances take thousands of years to evolve and mature), and in our lifetimes we can effectively work toward a goal of optimizing the sense of community on this planet. Creating environments that celebrate our individuality while at the same time maximizing social harmony is a vision worth embracing. It can include interaction with spiritual forces that animate the dream of beings learning to truly love each other.

Moreno recognized that the social structure was in need of healing as much as the individual. Psychodramatic methods and group techniques were created to be effective approaches for treating both entities. Moreno even proposed a meta-medical field called sociatry to address the dual nature of the challenge. It has actually evolved into applied social psychology; the mainstream of psychiatry has yet to integrate the wisdom of this vision.

Sociatry suggests an intriguing idea: What if we start treating the "diseased" elements in our society with a holistic approach?

That is, first of all consider "them" being related to "us." For instance, a holistic attitude toward our own burning stomach or aching head requires that instead of overriding these signals from our body by treating the symptoms with medicines, we commit ourselves to investigating the basic problems: Diet and life-style are the most common causes of the aforementioned disorders. Treating oneself with constructive action, encouragement, and conscious, gentle thoroughness will bring healing results. In the same way, social problems could be treated by methods for promoting collective catharsis (releasing destructive feelings and opening to healing alternatives). This was one of Moreno's visions for the use of the sociodrama that offers not so much abreaction as discoveries for integration.

This concept is not designed to offer a "cure," but rather to emphasize the importance of developing a theory and method that address the social as well as the individual sources of emotional and spiritual malaise. The advancement of sociatry will take time and will involve a lot of experiential experimentation. Philosophically, as professionals who are purportedly committed to aiding mental health, we must include social health, for to do less is to be guilty of an embarrassingly limited view of reality. Moreno's work offers vast resources for exploring and treating the needs of both areas.

At this point, it is also helpful to remember that psychodrama is only a part of Moreno's thought. The approach evolved from a metaphysical basis whose philosophical system is similar to that of Whitehead, as mentioned above, and other contemporary thinkers (Haught, 1984). Because of this, psychodrama is also meant to be used beyond the medical model, in education, spiritual development, politics, the arts, and other areas. It was this larger vision that prompted Moreno to begin his most revealing work, *Who Shall Survive?* (1934), with the ambitious, yet appropriate, statement: "A truly therapeutic procedure cannot have less an objective than the whole of mankind" (p. 1).

Psychodrama and its related approaches of sociodramatic play, sociometry, group dynamics, and others are methods that encourage the authenticity of the person by allowing for self-expression, not only in ordinary roles but also in the realms of imagination. These become valid channels for the development of aesthetic and spiritual parts of our human nature. In addition, the psychodramatic complex of methods encourages the evolution of group procedures and social organizations, which can create even more beauty on a collective basis.

In summary, the philosophy of psychodrama is based on a recognition that spontaneity is a primordial force, a source of nonconservable energy, and an essential component of creativity in the universe. On a human, social level, this emphasis suggests a belief in the maximization of individual and collective human potential when people are given the opportunity and have the skills to encounter one another—to communicate openly, honestly, and in the here-and-now. This approach is also similar to Habermas's theory of communicative praxis (Honneth et al., 1981). Moreno's methods of sociometry, psychodrama, and group psychotherapy, and his theories of spontaneity and creativity, thus emerge from a philosophically holistic orientation regarding the nature of what it means to be fully human (J. Moreno, 1976).

REFERENCES

Alexander, Franz, & French, Thomas. (1946). *Psychoanalytic therapy.* New York: Ronald Press.

Blatner, Adam. (1985). Moreno's "process philosophy." *Journal of Group Psychotherapy, Psychodrama and Sociometry, 38*(3), 133–136.

Blatner, Adam, & Blatner, Allee. (1987). *The art of play: An adult's guide to reclaiming imagination and spontaneity.* New York: Human Sciences Press.

Bromberg, Walter. (1959). Commentary. In J. L. Moreno (Ed.), *Psychodrama* (Vol. 2, p. 59). Beacon, NY: Beacon House.

Hartshorne, Charles. (1983). *Omnipotence and other theological mistakes.* Albany, NY: SUNY Press.

Hartshorne, Charles. (1984). *Insights and oversights of the great philosophers.* Albany, NY: SUNY Press.

Haught, John F. (1984). *The cosmic adventure.* New York: Paulist Press.

Honneth, A., Knödler-Bunte, E., & Widmann, A. (1981). The dialectics of rationalization: An interview with Jürgen Habermas. *Telos, 49,* 5–31.

Jentz, Arthur H., Jr. (1985). *Whitehead's philosophy: Primary texts in dialogue.* Lanham, MD: University Press of America.

Kazantsakis, Nikos. (1960). *The saviors of God.* New York: Simon & Schuster.

Kraus, Christopher. (1984). Psychodrama for fallen gods: A review of Morenian theology. *Journal of Group Psychotherapy, Psychodrama and Sociometry, 37*(2), 47–64.

Moreno, J. L. (1934). *Who shall survive?* Washington, DC: Nervous & Mental Disease Publishing Co.

Moreno, J. L. (1971). *The words of the Father.* Beacon, NY: Beacon House.

Moreno, J. L. (1972). The religion of God-Father. In Paul E. Johnson (Ed.), *Healer of the mind: A psychiatrist's search for faith* (pp. 197–215). Nashville, TN: Abingdon.

Moreno, Jonathan D. (1976). Psychodrama, phenomenology and existentialism. In Lewis R. Wolberg, Marvin L. Aronson, & Arlene R. Wolberg (Eds.), *Group psychotherapy, 1976* (pp. 26–33). New York: Stratton Intercontinental Medical Book Corp.

Pruyser, Paul W. (1983). *The play of the imagination: Toward a psychoanalysis of culture.* New York: International Universities Press.

Wilber, Ken (Ed.). (1984). *Quantum questions: Mystical writings of the world's great physicists.* Boulder, CO: Shambhala.

Winnicott, D. W. (1971). *Playing and reality.* New York: Basic Books.

7

Spontaneity

With this chapter, a bridge between philosophy and psychology will begin. The concept of spontaneity occurs in both areas. Philosophically, as we have discussed, spontaneity deserves to be valued because of its function as the essential component of creativity. Psychologically, spontaneity refers to a subtle quality of mind rather than a neat category of identifiable behavior. Moreno defined this concept in several ways (Moreno, 1941, 1944), but there were some inconsistencies in his presentation (Aulicino, 1954). It is easier to understand spontaneity through example than by definition, and here are a few obvious instances of its presence in several situations:

- Improvisations in the playing of a jazz musician or in ragas from India.
- Unstructured, make-believe play of young children; also, much of their drawing, painting, and exploratory behavior.
- Parents playing with their infants or young children.
- A person trying out new ideas in cooking, on the spur of the moment.
- The singing of a mockingbird, the play of kittens.

- An animated conversation, the mutual discovery of two people falling in love.
- The inspiration of a poet, the impromptu sermon of a preacher.

Spontaneity need not be showy or dramatic; it can be unassuming. It can be present in the way you think, walk, look at nature, dance, or sing in the shower. Rather than being an all-or-nothing phenomenon (i.e., an act that is or is not spontaneous), it can be thought of as occurring to a greater or lesser degree in most activities. Even in relatively habitual, automatic behaviors there can be a seed of spontaneity, if nothing else, functioning *in potentia*.

When looked at closely, the essential qualities of a spontaneous act are an openness of mind, a freshness of approach, a willingness to take initiative, and an integration of the external realities and the internal intuitions, emotions, and rational functions. Spontaneity is not mere impulsivity or random behavior; there must be some intentionality toward a constructive result, whether aesthetic, social, or practical.

For Moreno, spontaneity/creativity was the central ingredient in the process of psychodrama and of healthy living. He defined it as a new response to an old situation or an adequate response to a new situation. In addition, he called it "a non-conservable form of energy." These should not be taken as complete definitions but rather indications of some important features of the phenomenon. For example, a response does not have to be successful to be spontaneous, nor does its newness have to be obvious. It is possible for a pianist to play a piece for the hundredth time yet experience it and express it in new ways, with new subtleties of timing and emphasis. The same pianist could play it with little or no spontaneity, but the untrained ear might not notice much difference. This is the way in which it is a subtle quality of mind. Observers do not need to and generally cannot confirm that it is happening in someone else's life. Thus, it is not the act but the way the act is performed that reflects the inherent degree of spontaneity. It is manifest in proportion to the aliveness of mind and the utilization of what Moreno called "the category of the moment" as an opportunity for creative action.

It is interesting to note that there tends to be an element of surrender in spontaneity, as well as innocence, and this results in an expansion of consciousness. To do this in the present moment involves relinquishing excessive censorship in the mind's functioning, and it requires a corresponding opening to the inner impulses, intuitions, and inspirations. For example, remember a time when you danced to some music with a sense of abandon. For the most part, you probably recall it as some of your better dancing. Singing with gusto and enthusiasm produces similar results. Indeed, a good deal of the modern training of artists in various fields consists of freeing their spirit within the boundaries of mastering their medium.

Developing more spontaneity and creativity grows out of a basic relationship to the unconscious that is one of respect, openness, and delighted curiosity. The unconscious is not seen as a source of antisocial impulses but rather as a wellspring of insight, clues, hunches, images—in short, the reservoir of creativity. Accessing and using this innate creative potential is where psychodrama makes its greatest contribution. It accomplishes this by fostering conditions that evoke spontaneity: creating a relatively fail-safe context; introducing just enough challenge and novelty to create a little anxiety, a boost of energy to get things going; and maintaining a deep concern and respect for the problem at hand. Moreno used the term "warming up" for those procedures used to increase the participants' spontaneity, and that process will be described more fully below.

In Moreno's thought, spontaneity is the active expression of his existentialist philosophy. It is being receptive to the realities as they present themselves in the present moment, relatively unobscured by presuppositions. Even though we bring expectations and beliefs to every moment, we can change our attitude to one of experimentation rather than dogma, to a readiness to modify and correct our theories to adapt to present perceptions. This change will catalyze our spontaneity.

How we relate to our mistakes is a key element in spontaneity. The idea is to continue to improvise as an ongoing experiment, and instead of freezing, to turn a mistake into a "retake" that keeps the focus on the task. The state of mind developed by a samurai warrior in Japan gives a clue: "Expect nothing, be ready for anything." The spontaneous person handles interference by recentering and returning to a clear-minded presence in the here-and-now.

The dimensions of spontaneity are intimately involved in the wisdom of the East. Its subtleties and elusiveness are indicated in the narratives of students of Zen (Herrigel, 1953). While reading Robert Pirsig's book *Zen and the Art of Motorcycle Maintenance*

(1974), I was impressed that the essence of spontaneity fit the description of the elusive "Quality" sought by the protagonist and discussed at length, and was similar to something he also called "gumption."

It is interesting to relate spontaneity to the system of Yoga, in which there are generally seven *chakras*, each one corresponding to centers of consciousness located in various areas associated with the spinal axis. These areas also have been correlated with different types of psychological phenomena (Ram Das, 1974). Thus, the first *chakra* at the base of the spine reflects our basic concerns regarding security, the kinds of themes addressed by behavior therapy. The second *chakra* relates to sexuality and emotion, the kinds of themes addressed by Freudian psychoanalysis. The third *chakra* involves issues of power, as described by Adler's individual psychology. The fourth *chakra* encompasses functions of integration, the concerns dealt with in Carl Jung's system of analytical psychology. I propose that the fifth *chakra* relates to spontaneity, to the kind of inspiration of prophets and poets, the arena addressed by Moreno's psychodrama. The sixth and seventh *chakras* reflect transpersonal forms of psychophilosophy and practice. All of these dimensions are present in everyone, although some areas are more conscious and developed than others. Each *chakra* is considered an integral part of the whole, and all function together in a healthy system. In other words, it is not a hierarchical ladder in which the "higher" elements are better than the "lower" elements, a view that would distort the concept into a formulation more representative of Western thought. Imagine the *chakras* as a model of dynamic process.

Spontaneity develops through the ability to open to, rather than block or distort, the lower four *chakras*. It is part of the process of psychodrama to work on all levels of psychological issues to release the dynamic health of the whole system and to generate free expression of creative interactions.

SPONTANEITY VERSUS "ROBOPATHY"

Behavior that is automatic, habitual, fixated, compulsive, rigid, stereotyped, or practiced to the point of sterility is the opposite of spontaneity. These nonspontaneous behaviors comprise a good deal of what we call psychopathology. On a social level they take the form of prejudice, rigid policies, bureaucracy in its worst sense, and the most obsolete elements of tradition.

A syndrome involving the polar opposite of spontaneity was described by Lewis Yablonsky in his book *Robopaths* (1972). He presented in great detail the pervasiveness of restricted perspectives, compulsive gratifications, and a variety of other social pathologies. A robopath is someone whose basic dynamic is an unwillingness to take responsibility for engaging in new possibilities. Yablonsky noted that these qualities could be found on the collective as well as the individual level. Moreno had as one of his goals the development of the social system's capacity to encourage rather than discourage the creativity of the individual.

Moreno originally used the designation of the robot or machine to represent the opposite of perfect spontaneity. I think this is a somewhat misleading metaphor. It is more useful to consider that any pattern of fixated, habitual perceptions or behavior in our lives is an example of a relative lack of spontaneity. Any improvisation, on the other hand, no matter how apparently insignificant, is an example of a relative expression of spontaneity.

Of course there are places in life where habitual behavior is adaptive, such as in driving a car. However, even a little spontaneity is appropriate in order to cope with the unexpected when it arises. Similarly, in the arts and sports, mastering skills to the point of habit is the base from which spontaneous acts can emerge. This is one of the paradoxes of spontaneity: familiarity with the subject matter increases our capacity to play and improvise with it.

WARMING UP TO SPONTANEITY

A variety of theorists in the fields of communications and interpersonal psychology have noted that a paradox exists when someone is asked to behave spontaneously. This is because the phenomenon needs to emerge as part of involvement, like becoming more limber at the outset of a physical activity. In other words, warming-up is important in evoking spontaneity. Trying to will spontaneity is a paradox because the essence of this elusive quality arises out of the interaction between acts that are willed and functions of the psyche that cannot be willed. A shift of perspective is required, one that involves *allowing* rather than *forcing* things to happen. This is true in working and imagination, biofeedback, and other processes (Blatner & Blatner, 1987).

Moreno wrote about the way a boxer warms up by physically

beginning the activity of the match even before it starts. He also noted the importance of allowing this process to proceed gradually. This is a recognized principle in athletics and dance. Moreno noted Beethoven's warming-up process as he prepared to compose his music: He would pace up and down, waving his hands, making music in his mind and throat before he sat down at the piano. The physical and mental actions were inseparable parts of the whole process.

For example, I have a friend who is an amateur jazz musician and has become aware of a creative block in this endeavor. We reviewed the issues, and it became apparent that he did not know how to warm up to the creative process by starting with less creative activities and then progressing naturally. He had a sense that he should be able to plunge right into brilliant improvisations. Instead, he needed to warm up by playing melodic fragments, getting his hands and body moving and fooling around—trusting the process.

To trust the process is an important theme. It suggests that the "magic" of spontaneity can be reliably kindled given time and the proper receptivity to the unconscious. Of course, this requires a belief in the power of the workings of our inner selves. In the case of my friend's creative block, it became apparent that he thought "He"—that locus of control in the choosing self—was the creator, the source of the spontaneity. In some situations, the idea of cultivating that creator dimension of responsibility is appropriate, but it must be balanced with an understanding of when to allow the unconscious to exert its influence.

His thinking that spontaneity was something he could directly choose only increased self-consciousness and his block. We discussed the idea of allowing the unconscious to operate, permitting the "muses" to inspire his work. The locus of control might be permitted to shift to include sources beyond his ordinary sense of self.

The concept has practical clinical implications. Instead of expecting patients to come into groups or individual therapy sessions and immediately begin to address their problems in a meaningful manner, we should realize the need for time for warming up. Except for those few highly motivated patients who are already warmed up, some general digressions are not only permissible but desirable. A structured experience need not distract patients from their inner agenda, but rather it can heighten their awareness of conflictual themes. Silence, the traditional analytic technique, is a warm-up of pure ambiguity, and the anxiety generated tends to lead to similar associations. There are many types and ways to warm up, and the creativity of the therapist is invaluable in this regard.

SOCIAL DIMENSIONS OF SPONTANEITY

The phenomenon of spontaneity is reflected in what the philosopher Martin Buber called the I–Thou relationship. What Buber was trying to communicate was a difference between what he called the I–It relationship, in which people are approached as if all there was to know about them is known and fixed, and I–Thou, in which people are related to with an openness to the potentials of creativity and mystery in their being.

Moreno's concept of encounter, developed in 1914, reflected a similar desire for more humanistic, authentic social relations. The kind of encounter he envisioned was one in which people would role-reverse to some extent so that the act of empathic cross-identification would expand their consciousness. This must be contrasted to the oversimplified practices in encounter groups 50 years later, where authenticity was attributed to mere emotional self-disclosure. In those groups people frequently failed to go beyond the self to a genuine consideration of others' experiences. This may be one reason why the groups were accused of fostering narcissism rather than social awareness.

The group context can function as an excellent laboratory for the most mature and inclusive social skills; moreover, the involvement in interpersonal and group processes functions as a major impetus for the emergence of spontaneity and creative behavior. Moreno's various sociodramatic and sociometric techniques may be seen as structured experiences that tend to generate the kind of norms and involvements that can facilitate authentic interactions. In other words, spontaneity in the social arena is the vehicle for more creative working together.

THE CHALLENGE OF THE COMING YEARS

There are a number of practical implications associated with a recognition of the importance of spontaneity. One is to encourage more informal imaginative play, in adulthood as well as in childhood (Blatner & Blatner, 1987). Activities such as creative drama, improvisational theater games, and creative art and music need to be integrated into more aspects of our schools, camps, clubs, and hospitals. Competitive and structured games should not dominate our approach to recreation. In the arts, more time should be spent in "doing it," with less emphasis on presentation to an audience. In therapy, methods such as psychodrama and the expressive arts offer useful vehicles for empowering patients by reinforcing their sense of creative potential.

Previously, I suggested that the works of Freud and Moreno were two aspects of a process of exploration—Freud made the initial discoveries and mapped the territory; Moreno developed the resources. This comparison could also be made regarding the objective of clinical treatment. At the beginning of this century, Western culture was imbued with a pervasive repression of sexuality and aggression. The achievement of Freud and his co-workers is that people now recognize the nature of this repressive phenomenon. Freud addressed the layer of repression in our culture whereas Moreno called attention to yet another layer: the fear and avoidance of spontaneity. (This was also the object of the existentialist philosophers and writers.)

Avoidance and inhibition of spontaneity are now so pervasive they are hardly noticeable, which was the case with sexual repression earlier in this century. There is still too much reliance on habit, fixation, tradition, and rigidified modes of thinking. The lack of spontaneity in personal and social situations that contributes to chronic boredom; social alienation, alcohol, cigarette, and food addiction; and other common features in modern life should be recognized as reflections of a way of thinking that is constricted by not accessing the natural functions of spontaneity. Parenting, therapy, management, education, the practice of the art of medicine, and many other similar endeavors can be greatly enhanced by appreciating the value and cultivating the benefits of spontaneity. This shift of attitude can increase the capacity of people in our culture to respond creatively to the challenges of our changing times (Meyer, 1941).

In summary, it is necessary to bring our capacity for being receptive to spontaneity to the challenge of understanding the nature and implications of this obvious and vital aspect of human experience (Kipper, 1967). Animals also exhibit spontaneity, and it appears that all life may participate in behavior that is really more spontaneous than random. As modern philosophy and science open to the integration of the intuitive and emotional dimensions, such speculations connect our endeavors with the greater flow of existence. This extension of our consciousness will be discussed in Chapter 8.

In closing, I will paraphrase Freud's goal of psychoanalysis—"where id is, there let ego be"—to include, where there are closets of the unconscious, let there be consciousness. And then I propose that Moreno's goal would be, where there is a constriction of spontaneity, let there be spontaneity!

REFERENCES

Aulicino, John. (1954). A critique of Moreno's spontaneity theory. *Group Psychotherapy, 7*(2), 148–158.

Blatner, Adam, & Blatner, Allee. (1987). *The art of play: An adult's guide to reclaiming imagination and spontaneity.* New York: Human Sciences Press.

Herrigel, Eugen. (1953). *Zen in the art of archery.* New York: Pantheon.

Kipper, David A. (1967). Spontaneity and the warming-up process in a new light. *Group Psychotherapy, 20*, 62–73.

Meyer, Adolf. (1941). Spontaneity. *Sociometry, 4*(2), 150–167.

Moreno, J. L. (1941). The philosophy of the moment and the spontaneity theater. *Sociometry, 4*(2), 205–226.

Moreno, J. L., & Moreno, Florence B. (1944). The spontaneity theory of child development. *Sociometry, 7*(2), 89–128.

Pirsig, Robert M. (1974). *Zen and the art of motorcycle maintenance: An inquiry into values.* New York: Bantam.

Ram Dass. (1974). *The only dance there is.* Garden City, NY: Anchor Press/Doubleday.

Yablonsky, Lewis. (1972). *Robopaths.* Indianapolis, IN: Bobbs-Merrill.

PART III
Psychological Foundations

8

Psychological Foundations of Psychodrama

Beginning with this chapter, the rationale for the use of psychodramatic methods in psychotherapy will be explored. The following concepts will be discussed in this and the next few chapters:

- Psychodrama is best understood as an impressively rich method that can be applied within a holistic and eclectic orientation to psychotherapy.
- Drama is a more mature extension of the natural phenomenon of play, and this capacity for symbolic manipulation of experience is an important variable in psychosocial healing.
- It is important to help patients feel empowered through the use of methods that develop activity rather than passivity.
- The more vivid the method, the more it raises hope and opens patients to their own creative resources.
- Psychodrama includes both ends of the support–insight continuum, in a metaskills-oriented educational approach.
- These methods attend to the challenge of helping patients

rebuild viable dreams for their futures as well as reworking
the meanings of their memories.

- The variety of nonverbal dimensions inherent in psychodrama
  allows for greater access to the unconscious and for a broader
  range of self-expression through sublimations.
- Other apparent conflicts and dualities of experience can be
  balanced, such as subjectivity and objectivity, imagination and
  rationality, and so on.

In following chapters:

- The various benefits of the group therapies accrue also to psychodrama, which was one of the first forms of group
  therapy.
- Psychodramatic methods can be utilized in the development
  of various ego strengths.
- This approach integrates both individual and social psychology because it works with the functions of roles in the interpersonal field.

THE ECLECTIC CONTEXT OF PSYCHODRAMA

Psychodrama alone is no panacea. I believe it must be integrated
with a variety of components of therapy; some of these include
time for rational discussion, group interaction, and activities done
alone or with family members (i.e., "homework"). Moreover, the
rationale for psychodrama also applies to other therapies, for an
eclectic, integrated approach to psychotherapy. The sheer number
of different forms of therapy—more than 200—serves as an impetus for seeking some synthesis, some distillation of the common
elements in this multifaceted endeavor (Norcross, 1986).

Kurt Lewin said, "Nothing is so valuable as a good theory." I
believe a theory exists that can integrate the other theories, a modified form of role theory I call role dynamics (to be discussed in
Chapter 10). Psychodrama is a therapeutic method that can
operationalize this theory; and in helping patients learn to shift
roles, different aspects of a problem can be explored and more creative solutions developed.

For instance, role dynamics reverses the reductionistic efforts to
find ultimate "basic motivations." It celebrates the varieties of
pleasure and works to help people refine and diversify their aims.

Thus, the scores of theories of motivation (Madsen, 1968, 1974) and scores of theories of psychodynamics may not have to compete for a single victor. Rather, consider them to be ways of viewing the rich tapestry of human experience. As an analogy, the challenge of truly understanding history, beyond a mere chronology of events, involves the study of the historical implications of geography, agriculture, economics, linguistics, sociology, art, technology, political science, religion, philosophy, and the psychohistory of key people, as well as other variables. In psychology, the dimensions of neurophysiology, communications, cultural influences, temperament, and many other variables require an equally multidimensional approach. In therapeutics also, an eclectic orientation is appropriate. An analogy to medicine is appropriate, because in addition to the prescribing of various drugs, a modern physician might also perform surgery or manipulation or recommend special exercises, diets, mechanical aids, radiation treatments, and so on.

In psychotherapy also, a comprehensive modern approach to diagnosis and treatment should make use of the range of methods available to the practitioner (Beutler, 1983). Of course, these should be applied on the basis of some plausible rationale, rather than simply being thrown in when nothing else seems to be working—the practice that gave eclecticism a bad reputation. The problem was also that no theoretical system could account for the range of treatments, but this has been changing in the last few decades. For example, Lazarus's multimodal therapy (1981) addresses a number of facets of the patient's life: behavior, affects, sensations, imagery, cognitions, interpersonal relationships, and the need for drugs (if indicated) as a way to modify the neurophysiologic functioning. Lazarus uses a variety of techniques, and psychodramatic methods could be applied in correcting imbalances or distortions in any of the aforementioned categories.

THE PLACE OF PLAY IN PSYCHOTHERAPY

A fundamental part of human nature is the capacity to play, to juxtapose different, even paradoxical dimensions of awareness, with a resulting sense of delight, humor, and/or insight (Blatner & Blatner, 1987). By shifting among levels of awareness, a kind of transcendence occurs, an identification with the observing self rather than with the roles directly involved in the situation. Moreover, the sense of oneself as the observer may be subtly connected to something greater than oneself, such as the drama of humanity, the poetry of life, or the spiritual journey.

In psychodynamic terms, this playful process involves a realm that is neither autistic subjectivity nor absolute objectivity (as if that were possible). Winnicott (1971) calls this "the transitional space"; it is the relatively fluid dimension where people can utilize the potentialities of their imaginations. It is more explicitly expressed in drama, which allows it to be more consciously manipulated and yet less insidiously influential. Knowing an activity is a form of play makes it safer and thus accessible to creative risk-taking.

Play is a process used by children, not only for recreation, education, and self-expression but also for a natural form of healing. Allowed to engage in make-believe, even without any interpretations whatsoever, many children will symbolically work through a variety of mild to moderate conflicts. The power of a symbolic resolution must not be underestimated. In many situations, a dramatic, poetic, or artistic synthesis functions to shift the sense of involvement to a different level of meaning. Reexperiencing what was actually a defeat by engaging in a different, more victorious outcome results in a reduction in injury to the self-esteem and reaffirms the sense of optimism.

Another function of play is to reduce cognitive dissonance through finding imaginative solutions. Much of humor can be thought of in this respect (Mindess, 1971). Finding a meaningful gestalt in the face of a seeming impasse leads to a catharsis of relief, accompanied by laughter, tears, or other spontaneous behaviors. In psychodrama, even actions in the realms of impossibility (which Moreno calls "surplus reality"), such as an encounter with a relative who has died, can result in a powerful new internalization of a positive feeling–image complex, as well as feeling unburdened of previously unfinished affects.

All psychotherapies utilize the possibility of "as if." Psychoanalysis invites patients to engage in a degree of pretense in entertaining fantasies that would ordinarily be suppressed. Psychodrama simply amplifies this dimension, utilizing techniques that stretch the imagination while at the same time empowering the individual to choose, redecide, and create. This method offers role distance, which facilitates creativity, and it also encourages a dynamic dialectic with a state of authentic involvement (Moreno, 1966). This is especially important when the patient is being helped to engage another in an act of encounter. In psychodrama, opportunities exist to shift between the relative extremes of overinvolvement and underinvolvement.

ACTIVITY IN PSYCHOTHERAPY

The process of psychotherapy should not be thought of as a passive treatment in the sense of the medical model typified by receiving penicillin shots for pneumonia. Rather, it is a form of experiential learning, requiring a significant degree of courage and active participation on the part of the patient. However, one of the common aspects of psychological disturbances is a tendency to relapse into relative passivity. Patients frequently use the social status of the sick role to avoid exploratory and risk-taking behaviors.

One aspect of the healing power of all kinds of psychotherapy is that they involve the patient in a participatory activity, combining elements of imagination, emotion, physical movement, and cognition. This is true also of medicopsychological treatment in other cultures. Hypnosis, play therapy, biofeedback, psychoanalysis, rational–emotive therapy, psychodrama—all generate a role for the patient to play, and the patient's mental constructions in assimilating the belief systems of the therapist are part of the healing. Part of the nature of disease is the patient's uncertainty about the meaning and anticipated outcome of the process. Thus, jointly "discovering" a diagnosis, a process of creating an understandable theory that applies to the situation, is itself part of the treatment.

The relatively passive and seemingly inactive approach in psychoanalysis has influenced the field of psychotherapy to such an extent that activity on the part of the therapist must be rationalized. It should be noted, then, that psychoanalysis is actually quite active, but this activity is focused on a subtle, primarily verbal dialogue. It is a technique for reducing distractions and facilitating concentration. Other techniques are now available that can achieve these goals, and indeed they offer the additional benefits of including the innate need for physical self-expression, which is an integral part of a person's real-life functioning.

Moreno noted that there is a kind of "action insight" that accompanies effective psychodramatic procedures, and this often is more powerful and enduring than verbal insights. The involvement of physical, interactional, and spontaneous processes functions as a rich matrix for psychological syntheses. It makes it far more difficult to defend against an experience by means of isolation of affect, undoing, rationalization, or other mechanisms that reduce the emotional impact of an emerging insight. Furthermore, there is also generated a multimodal kinesthetic memory that functions spontaneously to remind a patient of new insights. The patient engages in an action that is visible to others, and this is even more powerfully validated when there is more than one other person present.

We must differentiate the concept of enactment, or therapeutic acting out, from nontherapeutic or antitherapeutic forms of acting out. When behavior is encouraged and subject to the influence of the group and the therapist, self-expression can include in turn both regressive tendencies and their corrective alternatives. The context's capacity to go along with the behavior subtly generates a degree of role distance that calls into operation the patient's observing ego. Thus, psychodrama utilizes the patient's "act hunger" to further the process of exploration in the same sense that a practitioner of the Japanese martial art of aikido uses the other person's energies to deflect an aggressive attack. Physical contact, encouragement, rescue, modeling, expressions of appreciation, play, humor, and many other elements all have a place, yet all must be used with judgment (Hammer, 1973).In child therapy, many patients require activity on the therapist's part (Jernberg, 1979), including behaviors that are intrusive, challenging, limiting, educational, and stimulating as well as the more recognized functions of nurturance and abiding.

VIVIDNESS AND VITALITY

The spirit of psychodrama goes beyond merely being a useful group of techniques. It reintroduces the issue of vitality and intensity and offers what Rousseau suggested, a method for helping people to relate on a level that results in a greater degree of expressiveness and closeness. In this atmosphere, connections and impressions can be more vital, and communications have enough emotional texture so that feeling and knowing become one (Hammer, 1980).

Poetry offers this, as do other expressive arts. In psychodrama, these forms can be integrated with nonverbal, actional elements—gesture, expression, tone, pacing, inflection, and the like. Psychodrama also adds to the richness of the artistic experience by giving the protagonist an audience, supporting actors, and a co-director, while also helping the protagonist to participate as a co-playwright. What is portrayed, as Moreno notes in speaking of "the theatre of truth," is not only what has happened but, even more important for the psyche, what could never happen—yet is nevertheless wished, feared, or wondered about. In addition, the experience of self-expression can be enhanced by artistic props. Musical pieces can be chosen or songs composed, combining poetry and melody. The whole event may be orchestrated with the sensitivity of a choreographer. The integration of the arts therapies has tremendous potential (Bruscia, 1986).

Another exciting element of improvisational dramatics is the challenge of becoming as spontaneous as possible. This involves the maintenance of a delicate balance, allowing unconscious material to flow to the surface, reducing self-consciousness to a minimum, and yet retaining enough self-possession to be creative and socially adequate and to remember one's process. (Of course, this requires the minimizing of social expectations by creating a protected context wherein greater extremes of emotion than are ordinarily expressed can be portrayed.) A further benefit of this multimodal approach is that it offers a source of mystery and surprise, mixed with the risk-taking and catharsis of courage that comes with trying something new. The delight and wonder at spontaneous behavior generates not only an enthusiasm for the activity but also an increase in the sense of positive expectation.

In the past, the therapist acted like a shaman, and the mystery of authority, education, and esoteric knowledge added a degree of charisma to the role (McNiff, 1979). Contemporary society has become far more egalitarian, and indeed criticism of authority is so pervasive that it is now often more therapeutic for the therapist to seek to demystify the process. However, this can make an interaction so mundane that vital elements of healing are lost. Working with the creative potential within the patient identifies a new source of charisma and hope. The challenge is to raise people's expectations of getting better, and this is enhanced by emotional arousal, the therapist's prestige, and an expanded level of symbolic communication (Frank, 1986). Drama as an integration of the other creative arts draws on the prestige of the arts throughout our culture and offers a multilevel channel for communication far richer than simple verbal dialogue. The arts become vehicles for affirmation, metaphorical constucts that are woven into the emerging, consciously rechosen "ego ideal." Our self-image is expressed in how we dress, move our bodies, and decorate our homes and offices; we can add to these symbols by creating stories, pictures, and poems about our experience.

Poetry and the arts regulate the inevitable psychic tensions that occur between the tendencies toward undifferentiated inclusiveness and differentiated preference. These two modes of experience have also been referred to as right- and left-brain thinking (Ornstein, 1972), as yin and yang, and in many other contexts. Burrow (1964) noted a similar differentiation between love and sexuality. When people allow themselves to be moved by beauty, a primary flow of emotion is opened, and this is experienced as a kind of transcendence. Identity shifts beyond the conventional boundaries of the self.

PSYCHOEDUCATIONAL FOUNDATIONS

Psychodramatic methods address both the insight and educational components of healing. Indeed, the idea of education resolves the apparent dichotomy between supportive and insight/expressive therapies. This is because the kind of education that occurs in psychodrama involves fundamental skills, which in turn require a maturation of the deepest attitudinal and emotional aspects of the psyche. I call them metaskills and include such categories as problem solving, communications, and self-awareness. An advantage of this orientation is that it helps to demystify the psychotheraputic process and strengthen the treatment alliance.

This educational approach also creates a model of treatment that demands more initiative and practice from the patient. Deep issues of resistance and transference can be addressed more effectively when the overall task is clearly defined. In a learning context, the attitudes of the student/patient must be addressed, as well as the simple communication of information; and in a skill-oriented approach, the learning must be through actual practice. This kind of experiential method is a powerful vehicle for bringing to the surface a rich variety of psychodynamic issues.

Insight alone is not enough for the majority of patients. The most common theme of insight is the experience of a basic sense of insecurity and vulnerability, along with a variety of mistaken beliefs, illusory goals, and modes of self-deception and manipulation that are used to protect the individual from the pain of the core sense of vulnerability. Yet the truth is that a number of skills and attitudes may be learned that can counter these fearful and shameful affects. Admittedly, patients' hopes for perfect gratifications and absolute guarantees of safety must be relinquished, but they are offered clear benefits that energize the process of making compromises. One reason educational approaches have not been more fully integrated into psychotherapy is that they have not as yet been systematically developed and/or taught on a widespread basis to practicing therapists.

To understand the way insight and education complement each other, consider an analogy between psychotherapy and gardening: Sometimes all that is needed to foster the optimum growth of a plant is some pruning, weeding, and elimination of harmful infestations. Factors that interfere with natural development are removed, and this could be analogous to the more analytic approach. Yet many plants also produce their best flowers or fruit if something is added—grafting, fertilizer, or even transplantation to a more congenial part of the garden. This could be analogous to education in therapy. Both approaches should be used as resources in individualized treatment plans.

SUBLIMATIONS: CHANNELS FOR SELF-EXPRESSION

Another primary principle of healing incorporates what I think is a vastly underrated concept in psychodynamic psychology: sublimation. Considered a healthy defense mechanism in psychoanalytic theory, it can seem beyond the role repertoire of ordinary people. Examples of sublimation often stress the productions of famous artists or scientists. Work with spontaneity, however, has shown me that we all are sublimating frequently, in small ways. Each act of style, originality, creativity, or the inclusion of elements of aesthetic flair functions as a sublimation. Adding a level of awareness or spirituality to an everyday action transforms it, helps it attain a dimension of transcendence. These qualities infuse the simplest of activities and should not be understood as confined to the province of the major arts and artists.

The function of sublimation plays a key role in helping us to understand how psychodrama works. According to my theory of role dynamics, an activity will be avoided if it is associated with feelings of vulnerability; thus, more immature behaviors might be retained if no support is given for the gradual and pleasurable acquisition of the new role. Applying this theory to the process of psychotherapy, I think that one of the major sources of resistance (in the broadest sense of attitudes or behaviors that interfere with personal growth) lies in patients' not knowing how else to channel their energies or achieve satisfaction, and a kind of stalemate results.

Because a significant source of resistance in psychotherapy is the patient's intuitive fear that there is no way for discovered feelings to be expressed or dealt with in a socially appropriate or effective fashion, some vehicle is needed for relieving this anxiety. Psychodrama offers the vehicle in the form of a relatively fail-safe "laboratory" for admitting the entire range of attitudes and affects. Expressed in the dramatic and therapeutic context, they are thus given a measure of new meaning: These expressions are reframed in their historical context as efforts used to work out problems rather than as evidence of intrinsic "badness." Thus, not only are creative actions encouraged and experienced in reworking the memories involved or the negative expectations that were feared, but also patients are helped to identify with a process greater than their own egos, which is the essence of transcendence (Frankl, 1978).

Role dynamics as I have designed it offers an approach to psychotherapy and education that develops the patient's or student's capacity for spontaneity and initiative in a variety of channels of self-expression. In a way, this is similar to the more holistic education in classical Greek culture, which consisted of areas that are often considered frills in today's educational philosophy. The goal of education in classical Greece was not the acquisition of information. Education was more process-oriented and led students into forms that promoted individual creativity, such as dance, music, drama, and rhetoric. Drama, especially the process of role-taking, is an important aspect of healing through active participation, visualization, and involvement.

The creative arts therapies, psychodrama, and other aspects of psychotherapy can and often do utilize the development of channels of sublimation as vehicles of treatment. Simply stated, when patients find something socially valuable to do with their energies and modes of self-expression that receives validation and generates pleasure, they are far more likely to relinquish patterns of belief and behavior that have become maladaptive. Role dynamics as I have envisioned it helps people to access a broader range of pleasurable possibilities, celebrates the diversity of the personality, and redirects patients to focus on their strengths rather than their weaknesses.

INTEGRATION OF PAST, PRESENT, AND FUTURE

Psychoanalytic approaches tend to emphasize the past; Gestalt therapy emphasizes the present; Adler's individual psychology addresses the idea of the future, insofar as his teleological approach examines the purposes and unconscious expectations of the patient. Psychodrama can enact scenes or amplify experiences in all three periods. By replaying the past in the present, all of the resources of the intervening time and surrounding social supports become available, and the individual is helped to become liberated from the fixated attitudes and emotions associated with traumatic memories. Positive aspects of the past can be recalled and reclaimed, reprojected as renewed future goals.

The present moment is a powerful category in Moreno's psychology and philosophy. It is an existential idea, a deep appreciation for the sense of creative potential. In becoming more aware of the here-and-now (a term Moreno invented around 1914) individuals are helped to engage more authentically in activities that increase their sense of being alive.

The future is an equally important dimension in psychodrama. The technique of future projection, the idea of role playing as a form of "rehearsal for living" (Starr, 1977), operates not only to develop skills and effective coping strategies but, more importantly, to help patients to reenergize their hopes and dreams. For many patients, the future is as repressed as the past. Desires for gratification are denied, and a subtle form of uncaring occurs that saps the energy of the personality. There is even a term for the part of the self that "amputates" these natural needs—the "anti-libidinal ego" (Guntrip, 1968). Thus, therapeutic efforts at restoring awareness of the future and clarifying and making realistic a variety of goals is a most powerful tool in treatment. (Allied to this is an analysis of the range of patients' goals and the vitality of their hopes and dreams as a valuable part of effective diagnosis.) I believe that an equal amount of work in psychotherapy should be done in building a viable sense of the future as is done in gaining insight into the past. This needs to be interwoven with an ongoing program for increasing the capacity of patients to learn to enjoy and become more aware of the present.

SUBJECTIVITY AND OBJECTIVITY

The contribution of phenomenology in philosophy has been to counter the excessively positivist and materialistic trends that were being promulgated in the late 19th and early 20th centuries. The validity of subjective experience has also been an important aspect of psychodynamic and existentialist psychotherapy. Yet the challenge remains of cultivating patients' skills of reality testing. I am not referring here to the gross abilities that become impaired in major psychoses, the loss of a capacity to differentiate delusion and hallucination from consensual reality. More important is the subtle and pervasive problem of characterological denial, the limitation of consciousness imposed by a prideful unwillingness to test reality, to check out one's own "private fictions" (as Adler called them) with other people.

Psychodrama uses the group context to foster feedback and, more important, the norm and value of asking for it. It further offers a variety of techniques to increase others' disclosure, such as the "behind the back" or the "mirror" techniques. (The latter is a nontechnological way of doing what is done in videotape playback.) Other techniques give feedback in the form of logical consequences, discovered by playing out fantasies and goals. Patients can carry dreams and suicidal ideations to their culminations—of course, this has to be done with discretion—and discover thereby the unconscious fantasies implicit in these symbolic expressions as well as their actual results.

In this regard, however, both subjectivity and objectivity become balanced in another dialectical process. Before people are ready to take on more socially "correct" role behaviors, they must first discover and express the unconscious ideas and impulses that seek expression. There is a kind of "act hunger" in the need to triumph over persecuting others, whether delusional or dream figures or actual people in the patient's past. This principle is well known in play therapy with children. A catharsis of owning the experience of a sense of mastery is necessary before the person can admit and feel the fullness of his vulnerability.

For example, Zerka Moreno has pointed out that in dealing with children many parents have a subconscious fantasy of an ideal child who has none of the problems of their actual offspring. If these can be portrayed and even experienced through role reversal, some differentiation can be allowed to occur between the psychologically internalized children one keeps close forever and the real ones who must inevitably be released into their own development and destiny. So, too, the grip in the psyche of a desired but unborn child (in cases of unresolved grief over an abortion or infertility) or of an unfinished goodbye with someone who has died or moved away; such internal psychodramas require a process of externalization so that the releasing power of the "higher self" can help in integrating the wish and the actuality.

Psychodrama's power lies in its bridging of the realms of imagination and rational objectivity, the desire and the realistic capability, omnipotent fantasy and the frustrating limitations of physical existence. By allowing for expression of the subjective world in a socially validated context, with the group as audience and the director as a facilitating agent, the person obtains at least a symbolic satisfaction; and this is functionally fairly effective in releasing the subtle repetition compulsions of fixated ideas.

INTEGRATING OTHER VARIABLES

Role dynamics addresses a variety of dimensions of human experience, which may then be explored and balanced using psychodramatic methods. In some situations a measure of confrontation is indicated; in others, the patient requires empathic support. The goal at one point may be an adjustment of oneself to a situation, an "autoplastic" focus—in contrast to an "alloplastic" focus, in which attempts are made to work out strategies for changing the environment or the behaviors of others. There are times in therapy for helping patients clarify what they already know inside, and other times for introducing new ideas. Depending on patients' needs, an enactment may be necessary to increase their engagement with each other; or perhaps it may work in the other direction and foster a process of separation and letting go (Blatner, 1968). There are many such dualistic variables in psychotherapy, and part of the diagnostic process involves an assessment of the nature of the imbalances and how to remedy them. It is this essential flexibility that accounts for the method's effectiveness.

In summary, the basis of psychodrama involves a number of issues: It is an approach that supports and is supported by the growing trend toward eclecticism in psychotherapy. The utilization of the innate tendency to play may be extended beyond therapy with children and adapted for the treatment of adolescents and adults.

Activity and the use of techniques that increase the vividness of the experience add to the empowerment of the patient. Including a skill-building orientation addresses deeper attitudes while sustaining the cognitive elements of the therapeutic alliance. Developing channels of self-expression helps generate healthy sublimations for previously uncultivated emotional needs. Emphasizing the future and applying methods for developing the capacity to create a more vigorous ego ideal is another important aspect of therapy. In all of these, the patients are helped to make more functional bridges between their subjective experiences and objective assessments of reality. These components offer significant additions to the range of therapeutic interventions and are thus relevant to the challenge of healing.

REFERENCES

Beutler, Larry E. (1983). *Eclectic psychotherapy: A systematic approach.* Elmsford, NY: Pergamon.

Blatner, H. Adam. (1968). Theoretical aspects of psychodrama. In *Practical aspects of psychodrama: A syllabus.* Thetford, England: Author.

Blatner, Adam, & Blatner, Allee. (1987). *The art of play: An adult's guide to reclaiming imagination and spontaneity.* New York: Human Sciences Press.

Bruscia, Kenneth. (1986). Perspectives on the creative arts. Keynote speech at the National Coalition of the Arts Therapies Associations Conference. *The Arts in Psychotherapy, 13*(2), 96.

Burrow, Trigant. (1964). In W. E. Galt (Ed.), *Preconscious foundations of human experience.* New York: Basic Books.

Frank, Jerome. (1986). Foreword. In I. Kutash & A. Wolf (Eds.), *Psychotherapist's casebook.* San Francisco: Jossey-Bass.

Frankl, Viktor. (1978). *The unheard cry for meaning.* New York: Simon & Schuster.

Guntrip, Harry. (1968). *Schizoid phenomena, object relations, and the self.* New York: International Universities Press.

Hammer, Emanuel F. (1980). Poetic, spontaneous, and creative elements in the therapist. In Arthur Robbins (Ed.), *Expressive therapy.* New York: Human Sciences Press.

Hammer, Leon I. (1973) Activity—An immutable and indispensable element of the therapist's participation in human growth. In D. S. Milman & G. D. Goldman (Eds.), *The neurosis of our time: Acting out.* Springfield, IL: Charles C. Thomas.

Jernberg, Ann M. (1979). *Theraplay.* San Francisco: Jossey-Bass.

Lazarus, Arnold. (1981). *The practice of multimodal therapy.* New York: McGraw-Hill.

Madsen, K. B. (1968). *Theories of motivation: A comparative study* (4th ed.). Kent, OH: Kent State University Press.

Madsen, K. B. (1974). *Modern theories of motivation: A comparative metascientific study.* New York: Halstead/John Wiley.

McNiff, Shaun. (1979). From shamanism to art therapy. *Art Psychotherapy, 6*(3), 155–162.

Mindess, Harvey. (1971). *Laughter and liberation.* Los Angeles: Nash.

Moreno, J. L. (1947). Varieties of psychodrama. *Sociatry, 1*(4), 221–224.

Moreno, J. L. (1966). The roots of psychodrama. *Group Psychotherapy, 19*(3–4), 140–142.

Norcross, John C. (Ed.). (1986). *Handbook of eclectic psychotherapy.* New York: Brunner/Mazel.

Ornstein, Robert F. (1972). *The psychology of consciousness.* San Francisco: W. H. Freeman.

Starr, Adaline. (1977). *Psychodrama: Rehearsal for living.* Chicago: Nelson-Hall.

Winnicott, Donald W. (1971). *Playing and reality.* New York: Basic Books.

9

Therapeutic Factors in Psychodrama

In addition to the themes mentioned in Chapter 8, the psychodramatic process partakes of a number of other therapeutic factors. One general category of these arises from the fact that psychodrama usually (but not always) occurs in a group therapy context. Thus, the variables found to be helpful in group psychotherapy also pertain to the benefits that can be obtained in psychodrama (Kellerman, 1984). Furthermore, because of the flexibility of the method, when certain factors seem to be particularly pertinent to a patient, they can be highlighted by using psychodramatic techniques. Let us examine this in terms of the curative factors mentioned by Yalom (1985):

Instillation of hope is a theme that is fundamental to all modes of therapy (Ehrenwald, 1976). This can occur by being in contact with others who have been benefited by the process, by meeting a therapist who has faith in the potential of the method to generate creative transformation or positive change, and by holding the expectation of help.

Similarly, discovering in a group the *universality* of one's concerns is a powerful source of support. A significant factor in psychosocial "disease" is that of demoralization, and part of this is the person's feeling of alienation, the belief that one's weaknesses and problems are relatively unique and shameful. Psychodramatic methods can help patients discover the breadth of common feelings involved in the human condition, and this stimulates its effectiveness.

Developing a sense of *altruism* in a group is an important element in healing because the aforementioned feeling of alienation also has roots in the tendency to become self-centered. In spite of some articles that have appeared in the last decade about how groups can be (mis)used to foster narcissism, the opposite is usually more accurate because people are encouraged to go beyond their habits of egocentricity and to consider in depth the needs and feelings of others. Psychodrama uses role reversal as a focused method for achieving this goal. The approach is an operational method for developing what Alfred Adler felt to be the most important attitude, *Gemeinschaftsgefuehl* (translated as "social interest" or "community feeling"). Adler thought this was the major alternative to the personal power strivings that he believed to be the basis of most psychopathology.

Contemporary medicine contains an instructional element, a belief that a certain amount of *information* is often useful in a holistic approach to healing. Group settings offer a good place to discuss a variety of principles of psychology, as well as other aspects of life.

Group psychotherapy also offers a *corrective emotional experience* by evoking some of the dynamics of the patients' early families and then allowing them to be worked out within a more conscious and supportive framework. Whether these are attitudes toward the therapist (as helper, authority figure, parent, teacher, or previous therapist) or toward other group members (as peers, rival siblings, or best friends) such transference phenomena can be clarified and corrected in the group setting. Psychodrama extends this process by making it more explicit, and as the early roles are reenacted by others, the reality of who they are in the group is enhanced. Perhaps the most powerful source of the corrective experience is the patients' co-creating scenes, wherein they experience the desired responses from figures from the past, which both validates the previously disowned feelings and empowers them to ask for what they want.

Another factor mentioned by Yalom (1985) is that of *developing socializing techniques.* Some of this will happen over time in the course of conventional group therapy that is limited to verbal discussion. However, psychodramatic methods that include the person's reenacting or rehearsing a scene brings out the rich dimension of nonverbal communication, including posture, gesture, and expression. Group therapy also offers specific techniques for constructively resolving conflict and for building the capacity for understanding oneself and others.

As part of the group process, participants may observe others' coping strategies and choose to practice *imitative behavior.* The benefits of modeling described by the psychologist Albert Bandura (1971) may be most directly pursued by using the technique of role playing as part of the group process.

A number of the aforementioned elements are combined in group therapy to offer a wealth of opportunities for *interpersonal learning.* A great deal is also acquired from actively participating in the process of a group co-creating more constructive norms and patterns of relating. Group members learn ways for more effectively expressing both positive and negative feelings and accessing multiple levels of insight.

Group therapy generates *group cohesiveness* by helping participants learn how to behave so that they can begin to feel accepted. "Belonging" is an important experience in therapy, generated through the development of abilities for cooperating in a group while continuing to discover and express one's own individuality. Success in this supportive setting cultivates the desire for social affiliation and the development of involvement in community contexts outside therapy. With the skills developed in "therapeutic" settings (in the broadest, educational sense as well as in the conventional understanding of the term), people may be more motivated and capable of engaging more constructively in other group activities, such as church, experiential education, politics, or even more wholesome family and neighborhood relations.

Group therapy also functions as a vehicle for *catharsis,* the emotional release that accompanies ego expansion and integration. By the use of psychodramatic methods, this process can be intensified, and the integrations that follow the cathartic experience may be consolidated. At certain points in group work, in spite of their weaknesses and in recognition of their creative strivings, patients may experience a catharsis when they feel accepted by the group. This "catharsis of inclusion" then functions to integrate socially the other constructive moves they have made in therapy (Blatner, 1985).

Finally, Yalom (1985) notes that group psychotherapy tends to confront patients with *existential issues*: the realities that life can be unfair, that there is no absolute escape from pain, and other recognitions of responsibility. Yet the group can also soften the message by offering the comfort of presence. An old hymn says it well: "You gotta walk that lonesome valley, you gotta walk it by yourself;/Ain't nobody gonna walk it for you, you gotta walk it by yourself." You may very well have to "walk it by yourself" in the existential sense, but that does not rule out someone's walking with you. It is this possibility of true human sharing that can do so much to reduce our sense of ultimate aloneness and contribute to the process of healing.

In considering the aforementioned themes, remember that some of the benefits of group therapy can be simulated by creatively using the "empty chair" when working with families, couples, classes, and even individuals. Other benefits of group therapy overlap with the healing factors in individual therapy.

Moreno developed psychodrama to be a social as well as an individual approach, and it achieves this dual role through the use of the group. By focusing on one patient in a group at a time, it addresses the individual's particular concerns; yet it uses other members as supporting players and involves the audience in giving feedback through action techniques, thus offering a great deal of benefit for others in the group. The power of the methods need not be confined to this kind of individual-centered motif; psychodramatic methods (in the form of sociodrama or role playing or in the context of using sociometric techniques) may be woven into a wide range of interchanges among people in order to explore a particular issue or facilitate resolutions of blocks in the group dynamics.

It is important to emphasize that Moreno was deeply committed to group psychotherapy. In the 1930s and 1940s, when the major psychotherapeutic approaches were confined to one-to-one interviews, he spent a good deal of time promoting the use of group work as well as developing psychodrama. For him, the two methods were seen as different aspects of the same system. Unfortunately, group psychotherapy could become incorporated into the mainstream of psychiatry only through the theoretical and methodological influence of the dominant system of the midcentury, psychoanalysis. This method tended to reduce the interactional and action-oriented components, focusing instead on transferential reactions to the therapist. In so doing, it lost most of its vitality. Only in the 1960s did it begin to open again to a more interactional mode and an emphasis on the here-and-now, Moreno's original intention. Also, the idea of action techniques could be entertained. By the 1970's, these trends had become mainstream, as reflected in the widespread acceptance of Yalom's textbooks (1985).

BEYOND THE DYAD

Psychodrama need not be confined to a traditional group context of 5 to 10 patients. The method can be used in individual therapy, including the technique of the empty chair. However, it should be noted that one of its most powerful advantages is the utilization of the natural tendency of humans to interact in small groups, three or four or five. The triangulations that arise out of these situations can be pathogenic if the roles tend to be fixed, and this dynamic is described frequently in the literature on family therapy. However, there is also a constructive use of triangulation, consisting of a flexible use of alliances combined with an explicit commentary on how the group process is relevant to the situation. This approach offers a degree of mutuality (as discussed in Chapter 8) not found in many situations.

Instead of having the third or fourth parties play a passive, observing role in the presence of an interaction between a patient and a therapist, these people are included as witnesses, mediators, advocates, doubles, auxiliary egos, and assistants to the therapists or patient in confronting one another. Moreno (1959) noted the power of this modification in reducing many of the complex transferential issues in therapy (p.236).

From a developmental perspective, this approach also has the advantage of helping patients make the bridge from being able to deal with one other person at a time to being able to deal with two or three others, which is part of what the universal dynamic of the oedipal conflict is about. Many forms of manipulation involve a dyadic relationship, and the presence of a third person can serve to undercut many of these destructive interactions. Psychodrama's emphasis on examining the process as well as the contents of the therapy tends to highlight the patient's interpersonal attitudes and behaviors. Including a third person as an auxiliary, playing roles of therapist, father, or other significant others in the patient's life, can intensify the emotions, bring out the transferences, and allow for a more flexible approach to their examination. Then these auxiliaries may also be used to explore more authentic encounters between the patient and significant others, both present and absent.

STRENGTHENING THE EGO

Another way of thinking about how psychodrama is effective is in terms of psychodynamic ego psychology—it "strengthens the ego." S. R. Slavson (1955) listed this as one of the dynamics he thought of as common to all psychotherapy (the other factors being relationship, catharsis, insight, reality testing, and sublimation). In an important and constructive critique of psychoanalysis, Yankelovich and Barrett (1970) noted that one area of weakness in the analytic approach is its lack of methods for directly strengthening the ego. A clue to the kind of strength needed was noted by Kubie (1958), who pointed out that an important indicator of mental health was a person's flexibility of mind, a quality similar to what Moreno meant by spontaneity. Psychodrama and the use of psychodramatic methods offer a number of approaches to strengthening the ego, in part by increasing its flexibility. Although support, education, catharsis, and insight are by themselves usually insufficient to effect a sufficient treatment, psychodrama integrates these components and so promises a more holistic and comprehensive method. Using Bellak's scales of 12 categories of ego functions (Bellak, Hurvich, & Gediman, 1973), we can review the ways psychodrama can help in strengthening these dimensions:

1. *Reality testing* is augmented because, in the enactment, protagonists are required to check out their perceptions against the reality of the social consensus and the limitations of concrete portrayals. In spite of the freedom of the dramatic context, the concrete nature of physically portraying a scene counters the distortions introduced by the evasive maneuvers that are more probable in a purely verbal discourse. By shifting roles physically, inner and outer stimuli become explicitly distinguished. By allowing for a full expression of fantasy and dreams, they are thereby helped to become consciously differentiated.

2. *Judgment* is exercised through playing out situations to their logical conclusions. This interferes with tendencies toward denial. Temptations to take risks can be symbolically tried out in a relatively fail-safe context, thus helping to differentiate between those with major or minor consequences. Through role reversal, patients can be helped to recognize inappropriate social responses, learning to discriminate between intentions, however well-meant, and the impact of specific behaviors judged from another's point of view. Another theme is the differentiation between one's desires and realistic expectations. This can be practiced by being given the opportunity to satisfy the act hunger in fantasy and following this, to address the limitations in the probable alternatives at hand.

3. *Sense of reality*, the subjective feeling, serves as an indicator of some degree of personal ownership, will, and responsibility. It is the opposite of the state produced by subtle or significant defensive mechanisms of denial, depersonalization, and derealization. Instead of allowing for the disconnection of experience, psychodrama is particularly effective in integrating it because the method involves physical action and imagination, sensation and intuition, emotion and reason, intrapsychic and interpersonal dynamics, and so on. In choosing how to proceed in playing a scene, it becomes increasingly difficult to respond according to others' (supposed) expectations, so "as-if" tendencies are gradually replaced by more authentic and sustained components of identity. Again, through role reversal, patients are helped to differentiate between their own qualities, beliefs, and preferences and those of significant others.

4. *Regulation and control of drives, affects, and impulse* can be enhanced through symbolic expression in a catharsis of abreaction, followed by modification in more mature forms through using such techniques as role training. A "catharsis of integration" follows the abreaction, in that the patient is delighted and relieved to discover that what had been considered an unacceptable part of one's makeup can function as a valuable part of one's role repertoire. A variety of channels of sublimation can be developed and exercised, and the opening of healthy modes of gratification makes it easier to relinquish old, less adaptive patterns of thought and behavior.

Using a variety of scenes and situations, patients can be helped to encounter a broad range of emotions and behaviors in themselves; and in the course of spontaneity training, these can be modified to include reality testing and choice making. Instead of habitual patterns of reacting either with excessive inhibitions or outbursts of emotion-filled behavior, the person becomes familiar with the enjoyable mastery of a range of coping strategies.

5. *Object relations* are explored and practiced in gradually more complex form by using psychodramatic enactments and the help of others, who can evoke the patient's spontaneity through their own vivid reactions. Beginning with relatively subjective and symbolic portrayals of oneself in relation to the superficial qualities (i.e., "part objects") in others, patients are helped to transcend the barriers of egocentricity and to engage increasingly in recognizing and dealing with otherness. Role reversal can be introduced in graduated steps, and patients can be coached to sustain a supportive enjoyment of the sense of mastery in building a new skill. As patients become more flexible, they are exposed to confrontations (mild at first) by those playing the roles of other people in their lives. Eventually, they learn to empathize with those other people's points of view.

The frustration of learning that others have needs that might conflict with one's own can be compensated for by discovering that others are also capable of forgiveness, inclusiveness, generosity of spirit, and other positive qualities. Role reversal leads to the development of a more realistic and mature kind of trusting, one that avoids the pitfalls of either idealization or devaluation. In addition, this skill becomes a valuable aid in discovering and revising transferential distortions.

6. *Thought processes* are exercised in a dynamic setting in which a significant degree of concentration, memory, and attention is required, at least for more complex enactments. Psychodramatic methods can foster patients' thinking abilities through the exercise of shifting between abstract and concrete levels of meaning or between "play" and "serious" modes of action. Such activities help them to communicate more clearly and yet learn to use language in a more metaphoric fashion. Of course, techniques may be modified and simplified to adjust to the abilities of those who have undue difficulties in the area of cognitive functioning. Thus, while "classical" psychodrama may not be appropriate for developmentally disabled, demented, delirious, or floridly psychotic patients, structured actional techniques often tend to be more useful than purely verbal and nondirective approaches (Yalom, 1985).

7. *Adaptive regression in the service of the ego (ARISE)* is Bellak's term for the person's ability to use play, fantasy, intuition, humor, artistic imagery, and other components that arise out of the

subconscious realm of "primary process" as vehicles for creative living (Bellak et al., 1973). Psychodrama actively employs this ego function, and the more it is intentionally applied, the more fluid and focused it can become. In spontaneity, as Moreno defines it, intuitive impulses and inspirations are balanced with the powers of reason and aesthetic sensitivity; expressiveness is balanced with effectiveness; and primary process is balanced with secondary process.

8. *Defensive functioning* is an area of ego development that can by systematically worked with, introducing and explicitly demonstrating the effectiveness of more mature defenses, such as sublimation, suppression, compensation, affirmation, and re-evaluation. Modeling of problem solving by others fosters toleration of mild to moderate amounts of anxiety. The safety of the stage and group allows for clear and explicit demonstration of their dynamics. Reaction formation, undoing, counterphobic responses, isolation, displacement, projection, and other symbolic defenses may be enacted and neutralized by using doubling, concretization, and shifting aspects of scenes. Reframing defense mechanisms as habits of thinking facilitates replacing them with mature defenses and adaptations, which in turn can then be practiced, encouraged, and reinforced.

9. *Stimulus barriers* can be strengthened in psychodrama through exploration of a variety of distancing, buffering, and "soothing" techniques (Blanck & Blanck, 1979). Skills for "giving oneself room" by using warm-up techniques can be adapted to the individual's needs. Patients are "given permission" by the group to allow themselves mild lapses of attention or memory, to ignore certain external or internal stimuli, and to reframe tendencies to ascribe catastrophic meanings to mistakes.

10. *Autonomous functions* are exercised through developing confidence in spontaneous behavior. The more patients improvise, the more they discover greater creativity in themselves than they thought they had. The group tends to support and validate the successful aspects of personal expressions, so patients tend to build skills and confidence in their own resources. Indeed, the subtle letting go of self-consciousness and self-control that is part of psychodramatic enactment, when supported by the relatively protected setting of the group, evokes increasing trust in the flow.

11. *Synthetic-integrative functioning* is perhaps the primary dimension developed in a psychoeducational approach such as psychodrama. Use of the multiple-ego technique, in particular, can

help patients to experience and clarify the different parts of their personalities. By the fostering of a kind of internal encounter, a supraordinate "choosing self" emerges, one that, in the role of judge, big sister, spiritual guide, or another wise and helpful character, seeks compromises with new alternatives for the various internal conflicts.

12. *Mastery–competence* is an important dimension that may be enhanced through the kinds of behavioral practice found in role playing and psychodrama. The situations can be devised so as to offer a hierarchy of difficulty, and through the reinforcements of group encouragement, patients begin to experience a series of successes.

In addition to the ego functions, Bellak and associates (1973) noted some aspects of superego and drive (i.e., id) functioning, and these too may be worked with constructively in psychodrama. For example, superego distortions may be addressed more readily when contrasts with a freely chosen ego ideal are drawn. The future-projection technique allows goals to be clarified, and aspirations and values can be tested against at least a partial simulation of possible alternatives. Psychodramatic methods for evoking symbolic gratifications also help to modify excessive or overinhibited libidinal (e.g., sexual) or aggressive drives. Allowing for a protected kind of self-expression can redirect the immature feelings and aims in more socially acceptable channels.

In summary, psychodramatic methods may be seen as operating as agents for developing effective and more mature ego functioning. Some examples of this have been described, using the categories of Bellak et al. (1973). It should be noted that the other creative arts therapies can be understood as working in a similar fashion. In addition, as discussed elsewhere, these approaches may be applied directly in the analysis of intrapsychic and interpersonal problems.

REFERENCES

Bandura, Albert. (1971). *Social learning theory.* New York: General Learning Press.

Bellak, L., Hurvich, H., & Gediman, H. K. (1973). *Ego functions in schizophrenics, neurotics, and normals: A systematic study of conceptual, diagnostic, and therapeutic aspects.* New York: Wiley.

Blanck, Gertrude, & Blanck, Rubin. (1979). *Ego psychology II.* New York:

Columbia University Press.

Blatner, Adam. (1985). The dynamics of catharsis. *Journal of Group Psychotherapy, Psychodrama, and Sociometry, 37*(4), 157–166.

Ehrenwald, Jan. (1976). *The evolution of psychotherapy.* New York: Jason Aronson.

Kellerman, Peter Felix. (1985). Participants' perceptions of therapeutic factors in psychodrama. *Journal of Group Psychotherapy, Psychodrama, and Sociometry, 38*(3), 123–132.

Kubie, Lawrence S. (1958). *Neurotic distortion of the creative process.* Lawrence, KS: University of Kansas Press.

Moreno, J. L. (1959). *Psychodrama* (Vol. 2). Beacon, NY: Beacon House.

Slavson, S. R. (1955). Group psychotherapies. In J. McCary (Ed.), *Six approaches to psychotherapy.* New York: The Dryden Press.

Yalom, Irvin D. (1983). *Inpatient group psychotherapy.* New York: Basic Books.

Yalom, Irvin D. (1985). *The theory and practice of group psychotherapy* (3rd ed.). New York: Basic Books.

Yankelovich, Daniel, & Barrett, William. (1970). *Ego and instinct.* New York: Random House.

10

Role Dynamics: The Psychological Foundation of Psychodrama

In addition to his other contributions, J. L. Moreno was also one of the founders of social psychology and, along with George Herbert Mead and a few others, one of the primary developers of role theory. The idea of using the concept of role as a bridge between social and individual psychodynamics was obvious to Moreno, perhaps because it was associated with drama and perhaps because it fit so well with his theories of sociometry. Moreno's intention was that the concept of role could function as a tool in therapy, group work, and everyday life. However, in fact, role theory as an approach in sociology is essentially descriptive in nature (Biddle, 1979; Sarbin, 1966) and as such has become an academic, theoretical system. Moreno's viewpoint is more oriented to clinical application and more involved with methodology and is thus essentially different from the traditional sociological usage. (A recent sub-group, "clinical sociology," has emerged in the last decade, which may find a good deal of inspiration from Moreno's work.) I have integrated Moreno's ideas into a more expanded and systematic theory that I call role dynamics.

Role dynamics has a number of benefits as a general framework for psychology: It is holistic insofar as it addresses all of the dimensions of human experience. It can integrate other theoretical ideas and so functions as a basis for eclecticism in psychology and psychotherapy (as will be discussed further in Chapter 11). Its language is simple; even nonprofessionals can understand it. Thus, it serves as a tool for presenting psychological principles in an educational context. Roles tend to be described in terms that are somewhat balanced between the extremes of abstraction and concreteness, and thus these terms can serve as a useful yet vivid way for communicating psychological and interpersonal dynamics among professionals.

More important, role dynamics suggests a methodology. By naming our complexes of interactions, attitudes, and expectations, we create some distance from these roles, and thus they become somewhat objectified. We can examine them, renegotiate them, try out different ways of playing them, consider related roles and opposite roles, and so forth. In other words, the concept of "role" encourages us to become more conscious and creative in how we choose to play our roles, which was Moreno's basic idea. Also, one of the fundamental techniques that expresses the principles of role dynamics is that of role reversal, which functions as an effective vehicle for developing and communicating empathy. This is perhaps Moreno's most valuable contribution.

Incidentally, the way we use the term "role playing" is in the sense of an intentional and somewhat experimental act, neither wholly involved nor yet entirely inauthentic. Sometimes the term is used by other writers in the field to refer to a role enactment in which the person is fully immersed in a role, perhaps with no awareness of the possibilities of renegotiating that situation. I should prefer to call this "role living" (Horner, 1986) because there is little that is playful about it. The point is that to enhance the playfulness means to enhance freedom. One cannot escape from being in roles because this is simply a way of defining a relationship. However, it is eminently possible to increase the flexibility of these arrangements, to make them more negotiable, more varied, and even to exchange role components at times.

ROLE DISTANCE

Perhaps the most powerful feature of role dynamics is that the concept of role implicitly suggests a separation between a psychic identification with a complex of behavior and the potential of the self to choose alternatives. Instead of saying that one is stingy, for example, the person could be described as playing that role in a stingy fashion. The former attribution almost encourages a person to reply, "Well, that's the way I am, and I can't change." The latter approach encourages a person to be creative and to reevaluate behaviors in order to develop new possibilities (Landy, 1983). Berger (1975) notes that an awareness that we are playing roles allows for more freedom in our lives, because the position of standing outside—he uses the word *ecstasy*—provides enough distance to reconsider the subtle assumptions underlying our situation. It has implications not only for changing oneself but also for the subcultural and cultural norms and organizational structures. This, too, was Moreno's goal.

A movement toward this level of abstraction about our psychosocial activities has been a feature of the last century, and the concept of role (and the implications of role distance) allow for an operationalizing of this insight. It is analogous to the development of alphabetical writing instead of pictographic writing, the former permitting a far greater range of abstract thinking (Logan, 1986). Another way of thinking about this is that the relativistic frame of mind has come to be more appropriate for our changing culture, and theories such as Vaihinger's philosophy of "as if" have served as stimuli to more flexible approaches to psychology (i.e., Adler, for one, acknowledges this nonabsolutistic attitude as an influence on his pragmatic approach) (Vaihinger, 1935).

The concept of roles and the implication of role distance is not so abstract as to be impractical, however. Our familiarity with the experience of play and make-believe as children, and with the theater as a recognized part of culture, makes the idea of role playing easily understood by most people. The idea of shifting roles, which is the most useful part of the concept, is the essential idea underlying the way psychodramatic methods can be applied in a wide variety of contexts.

HOW ROLES CO-EXIST

Moreno (1960) described three major categories of roles: somatic, social, and psychodramatic. Somatic roles include such activities as eating, sleeping, style of dress, and personal habits. Social roles include occupational, economic class, racial, sexual, and family roles. Psychodramatic roles are those played in fantasy, such as dreams of having a wonderful marriage, a successful career, or an adventure. This category also includes all of the characters in your imagination, fictional figures, people in your memories or dreams, and your complexes of attitudes and behaviors. Moreno noted that in the course of normal development a child plays out psychodramatic roles as a way of preparing for social roles. In addition to the types of roles, there is a range of ways in which each role may be portrayed. For example, the role of lawyer may be portrayed in a belligerent or appeasing manner. A knight could be a comic or a tragic figure. A spiritual guru might be enacted as a seductive, arrogant or silly character. The ways are simply the range of adjectives and adverbs to flesh out the different nouns, the names of the roles.

In real life, a person is living within a complex comprised of many roles, operating on several levels of social organization and in relation to other roles. In learning the skill of role taking, however, usually only a portion of this complex is explored in order to highlight the emotional aspects of certain roles and to keep the experience within a manageable range. For example, imagine a scene of a family at a Christmas dinner (Nye, 1976). There are multiple levels operating simultaneously. Let us focus on just one of the people in the scene—say, the teenage daughter. On a somatic level, she is having her own dynamic experiences related to food preferences, concerns about her weight, and her tendency to be a very slow eater. On a social level, she is in subtle competition with a brother; in conflict with her father, who insists on smoking at the dinner table; and emotionally hungry for more attention from her much-loved visiting grandmother. In addition, she plays a role of peacemaker as others in the family interact with each other with varying levels of friction or harmony.

On a psychological level our imagined protagonist is also having her own inner conflicts. There are roles inside, such as the "provocative and rebellious daughter" who is being held in check by the "nice girl." In addition, there are cultural influences operating, such as ethnic background and religious traditions. There are even role relations that exist on a collective as well as an individual psychological level. For instance, there might be a general awareness that this is the first Christmas dinner that Grandpa has not attended; he died 4 months earlier, but he is present "in spirit." You do not have to be a Broadway playwright to realize the dramatic potential that is inherent in such a seemingly ordinary situation.

MORE ABOUT ROLES

As you consider the process of role-taking, consider the following principles:

- Roles are learned and can be revised.
- Roles can be lost, taken away, relinquished.
- One can vary, modify, and redefine many roles.
- Most roles are implicit or explicit social contracts; that is, the roles of parent, teacher, policeman, customer all require an agreement by others to behave in some reciprocal fashion.
- Many roles exist in relationship to other roles; that is, the role of son implies a parent; the role of king implies subjects.
- Conflicts or difficulties in adjustment often emerge as people engage in the dynamic processes of changing aspects of their roles—learning, redefining, renegotiating, or making transitions between major life roles.
- Every relationship consists of several roles. A marriage includes such roles as sharing money management, romance, social interests, child rearing, and so on. There are often conflicts among these roles that are built into the nature of most relationships.
- Many roles have subroles or role components. Sometimes there are conflicts between these component roles. For example, a mother needs to protect her children yet encourage their risk-taking.
- People usually have some conflicts among their various roles. For instance, a chef must plan his menu on the basis of both economic and esthetic considerations.

Awareness of these dynamic factors, the range of roles, and the different ways roles may be played all become clues for diagnosis or cues for helping the auxiliaries or directors in their work.

ROLE ANALYSIS

A diagnostic application of role dynamics involves an analysis of the varieties of roles and role components that are functioning in a given individual, relationship, or family (or small group) (Moreno, 1953, p. 293). Role analysis can be a powerful diagnostic tool, the relevance of which is immediately obvious to the patient. It deals most specifically with the interpersonal field because each role is explicitly or covertly agreed on between two or more people. In addition to an examination of the various key relationships in patients' lives, the different roles played also give a useful picture of their actual situations. Then, while reviewing a patient's role repertoire and considering the many different kinds of needs and motivations, one might keep the following questions in mind:

- Are some dimensions of the personality being suppressed? Is this causing problems?
- If some roles are expressing an excessive or distorted motivation, can the essential need be recognized?
- Might roles expressing one facet of the personality be overdeveloped in part because others are being neglected?
- Are there any important dimensions of personal development that are being repressed or denied, and could other actions express efforts to compensate for or disguise these needs?

Another way to help patients understand their situations is to use the technique of having them diagram their "social atom," Moreno's term for the network of significant others in a person's life. The social atom can reflect between 3 and 15 of the key figures. If patients have many more, it might be an interesting exercise to have them choose the most important ones. The others can be drawn as little circles (or other geometric figures), and lines may be formed to indicate whether the feelings toward each of the characters are positive, negative, or neutral. The perceived feelings of the other people may also be indicated.

Examining a single role within this network may also be a productive exercise, especially when that role is an important and multifaceted one, such as a spouse or parent. Each role component may be diagrammed (Hale, 1975). Often the role components may themselves require some breakdown into subcomponents; for example, in a marriage, the role component of housekeeping may require some analysis regarding such issues as who does what chore, how the decisions regarding this role distribution are arrived at, and who maintains the standards of adequacy in their accomplishment. Role analysis within families can reveal patterns of triangulation, such as in situations where the parents are allied in certain roles but compete (and perhaps are allied with one or the other of the children) in other roles. This helps explain inconsistencies in trying to establish fixed patterns in families.

However, most diagnostic processes are hindered by attempts to make global descriptions of behaviors that are in fact somewhat role-dependent. This type of role interaction analysis produces more material than simply deriving the patient's "lines of development"; moreover, diagnostic flexibility is increased. The point is that, as is well known, a child may be more regressed with the mother than when visiting at the home of a friend. This process can be used at many points in the course of psychotherapy. In living relationships, roles and their associated issues are dynamic and change noticeably as the situation changes. Thus, just as the tissues in a physical organism are far more dynamic in a living state than any microscopic picture based on a slice of tissue, dead and fixed with dye, so the components in a relationship are far more alive than any diagram can capture. They are continually changing form and intensity, growing, dying, evolving, merging, separating, and dancing.

It is often important to look for actual or implied third parties (and perhaps others also) because interpersonal dynamics are frequently more understandable from that perspective. This is part of the reason the psychoanalytic observation of oedipal dynamics is so common. Even if there are no obvious sexual issues or relational connections with parental figures, the key themes of having to deal with jealousy, shifting alliances, the role of audience (i.e., a person for two people to show off for), fears or feelings of exclusion, and the like are indeed universal phenomena. At about the age of 4 or 5 years, every child learns to deal with more than one person at a time.

In triadic relationships such as those found in families or among playmates, one can easily notice a shifting of alliances and the role of the audience. For example, at times A and B are together, with C feeling a bit left out; sometimes C and A might be the active pair—but always with an awareness of B's presence. In both dyadic and triadic relationship analyses, process issues also may be considered: how (or whether) consensus is achieved; the levels of seriousness or playfulness, rigidity or flexibility; caring about the other's feelings or egocentricity; and so on.

ROLE-TAKING—THE KEY SKILL

With the concept of role functioning as a focusing agent, we can learn to think about another person in a more efficient fashion. If I were to ask you, "What do you think it's like to be your brother?" (assuming you had a brother), you might respond that the question is simply too broad, and you would be right. People you know are composed of many facets, and it is often difficult to know where to begin. However, using the concept of role, we can begin to think of a person such as "your brother" in terms of major and minor involvements: his roles as father, brother, and son, his occupation, his main interests in life, and so one. Then each of these roles may be further examined in terms of their components. Which roles are chosen for this examination will necessarily reflect the special areas of concern of the person doing the exercise. It is excessive to attempt to understand everything; there are just too many aspects. The concept of role thus acts in a way roughly analogous to the use of lenses in astronomy or microscopy—to focus on specific aspects, one at a time.

The actual process of thinking about another person's role repertoire requires a mixture of imagination and rational extrapolation. This is the way the legendary Sherlock Holmes worked. He imagined a variety of possible scenarios and then used his logic to test out their probability and the probability of further inferences to be drawn from each line of thought. However, the initial activity was more meditative than focused; he allowed images to form spontaneously, and he remained receptive to this intuitional process. This is a mode of problem solving that is rarely taught in the course of ordinary professional education, but it is used widely by playwrights and the writers of novels. It is one of the major principles of role dynamics that psychotherapists learn to think this way also.

The difference between clinical psychology and psychiatry and the physical sciences must be repeatedly emphasized, because there is a pervasive implicit bias in our culture that science is the best way to deal with things. However, the limitations of science are only beginning to be fully recognized. The hierarchical elevation of science is a shallow form of scientism, and genuine scientists are unafraid of allowing their imaginations to participate actively in the generation of fresh hypotheses. In other words, I want to encourage therapists to dare to use their imagination and to indulge and cultivate their capacity to make inferences. This takes practice, especially if they have been immersed in a mind set that relates to psychology in terms of truth and error, right and wrong answers on tests, and other creativity-inhibiting modes.

When with a patient, the therapist can imagine him- or herself in that patient's role regarding a given situation. The mind can be open to the associations that are stimulated in that context. This is a more focused form of the free-floating attention advocated by the depth psychologists, yet it shares the same spirit. The therapist can then check out these inferences by asking the patient, "As I imagine myself experiencing that, I would also feel [such and such]" or "If that happened to me, I might be reminded of [so and so]"; and then he or she can ask, "Does any of what I said hold true for you?" It allows for and indeed even invites the patient to correct and modify the associations. The process of constructing a viable and meaningful hypotheses about the patient's experience then becomes a mutual task, which adds to the empowerment of the patient and the therapeutic alliance.

Another principle to consider in the role repertoire of patients is somewhat analogous to the second law of thermodynamics, namely, "to every action there is an equal and opposite reaction" (Carlson-Sabelli & Sabelli, 1984). This means that whatever role is being expressed, there is a likelihood that there is also an opposing tendency latent in the patient's personality. Thus, using this principle of role dynamics, consider possible scenes in which this other aspect could be brought forth, perhaps in a disguised form (e.g., a fictional role). People have a tendency to seek "role relief," consciously or unconsciously—a phenomenon in which a sense of release of tension or pleasure is experienced when a person can play roles that are radically different from those that demand a good deal of time in real life. In other words, people need to experience variety and balance and not get fixed in one role. Thus, if the therapist is aware of a patient's tendencies to control, he or she should listen for which roles in the patient's life might express some opposite interpersonal stance, such as serving, following, or obedience.

In the actual process of role playing in a group, observe how the behavior of the other participants (i.e., auxiliaries) influences the behavior of the protagonist, usually evoking either complementary or symmetrical reactions (Leary, 1957). For instance, if the protagonist is portraying a situation at work and the auxiliary plays the part of the supervisor with a rather authoritarian tone, the protagonist may be inclined to react by becoming either more intimidated or more rebellious. In this way the enactment also serves as a diagnostic instrument.

FURTHER THERAPEUTIC IMPLICATIONS

Bringing this back to clinical practice, the task of the therapist becomes not just registering certain clinical patterns in the course of diagnosing a case but rather developing empathy, a sense of what it is like to be the patient. This is one of the key components of what Carl Rogers called client-centered therapy, which he found to be a major element of effective therapy regardless of the therapist's theoretical orientation. Moreover, the open exercise of this process builds the therapeutic alliance and reduces resistances based on the fear of being misunderstood.

What if the imagined qualities are inaccurate? Sharing them openly and allowing the patient to correct them makes them more accurate; and, in addition, patients will feel the therapist is not going to come to conclusions about them without their consent. I frequently inform patients about the above issues early in the sessions; in this way they are introduced to the techniques of role-taking and role reversal and are encouraged to modify the emerging picture, which helps to reassure them about our process together.

Nor is there any loss of the therapist's authority in confidently using this technique. Instead, it is novel and refreshing enough to engage the patient's curiosity. It stimulates the patient's interest and curiosity and challenges the therapist to see if he or she can truly empathize with the patient, using words phrased so that the patient feels understood. This subtle, playful element can paradoxically communicate genuine compassion about the patient's distress while seeking to understand the dynamics and to formulate new strategies.

TEACHING PATIENTS ROLE-TAKING

The skill of empathic role-taking is certainly not limited to clinical settings. It can be used in everyday life, and it is a powerful technique in therapy to teach patients how to think this way in their own relationships. It helps to reduce egocentricity while at the same time giving a task that can be mastered with coaching. I am convinced that teaching role-taking and role reversal should be a significant component of family therapy, in earlier or later phases, depending on the judgment of the therapist. It is a way of making the golden rule operational and so teaches a life value as well as a skill.

In individual therapy, there are certain points where it is helpful to have patients understand the experience and motivation of significant others in their lives, past, present, or future. I have them sit in another chair (the empty-chair technique) and imagine being the other person. For example, if the patient—let's say, a man—was abused as a child and has carried with him a sense of shame/guilt because he felt he might have deserved the punishments, it could be helpful to have him play the role of the abusing parent. I then interview the "parent," perhaps the mother, and explore what was going on in her life at the time: the level of social support, previous childrearing experiences, opportunities to experience a happy childhood herself, and similar themes. Usually, what emerges is a picture of the abusing parent as overloaded emotionally and displacing onto the child his or her own sense of vulnerability and self-hate. In the aforementioned example, the patient is likely to access some information that helps in forgiving himself, and even perhaps a little insight into beginning to forgive the parent.

If patients do not have the information to answer the questions in role, this process directs them toward what kinds of additional history they need to get from family members. However, it is amazing how much people can reconstruct—more than they might think possible—once they are actually in the role. The art of interviewing for the therapist in this setting involves asking questions at the periphery of the issue at first and then warming them up gradually to the fullness of the other person's experience.

At this point I must state that the skills described above are best learned by doing the exercises and practicing them under the supervision of someone who is familiar with the technique. There is a bit of a knack to integrating imagination and more intellectual faculties, and, like catching on to the idea of swimming or riding a bicycle, it requires an experiential mode of learning. This can also be learned in a playful setting, and a number of techniques for developing the skills of role taking are described in our book *The Art of Play* (Blatner & Blatner, 1987).

In summary, role dynamics represents a clinically relevant form of role theory that invites both therapists and patients to think flexibly about the range of roles available for creative renegotiation or development. In spite of the way earlier psychologists and sociologists have tended to describe roles as fixed, overdetermined categories (Goffman, 1971; Moment & Zaleznik, 1963), Moreno (1960) pointed out that in reality they are tremendously flexible and capable of extensive, healthy, creative modifications (pp. 84–86). Learning how to generate a broader range of roles happens through dramatic play in childhood, and this may be extended as a tool to facilitate an ongoing development throughout life.

REFERENCES

Berger, Peter. (1975). Society as drama. In D. Brissett & C. Edgley (Eds.), *Life as theater* (pp. 13–22). Chicago: Aldine.

Biddle, Bruce J. (1979). *Role theory: Expectations, identities, and behaviors.* New York: Academic Press.

Blatner, Adam, & Blatner, Allee. (1987). *The art of play: An adult's guide to reclaiming imagination and spontaneity.* New York: Human Sciences Press.

Carlson-Sabelli, Linnea, & Sabelli, Hector C.(1984). Reality, perception, and the role reversal. *Journal of Group Psychotherapy, Psychodrama, and Sociometry, 36*(4), 162–174.

Goffman, Erving. (1971). *Relations in public.* New York: Basic Books.

Hale, Ann E. (1975). The role diagram expanded. *Group Psychotherapy and Psychodrama, 28,* 77–104.

Horner, Althea. (1986). *Being and loving.* Northvale, NJ: Jason Aronson.

Landy, Robert. (1983). The use of distancing in drama therapy. *The Arts in Psychotherapy, 10,* 175–185.

Leary, Timothy. (1957). *Interpersonal diagnosis of personality.* New York: Ronald Press.

Logan, Robert K. (1986). *The alphabet effect.* New York: Morrow.

Moment, David, & Zaleznik, Abraham. (1963). *Role development and interpersonal competence.* Boston: Harvard School of Business Administration.

Moreno, J. L. (1953). *Who shall survive?* New York: Beacon Press.

Moreno, J. L. (1960). *The sociometry reader.* Glencoe, IL: The Free Press.

Nye, Ivan F. (Ed.). (1976). *Role-structure and analysis of the family.* Beverly Hills, CA: Sage Publications.

Sarbin, Theodore. (1966). Role theory. In Bruce J. Biddle & Edwin J. Thomas (Eds.), *Role theory: Concepts and research* (pp. 488–567). New York: John Wiley.

Vaihinger, H. (1935). *The philosophy of "as if".* London: Routledge and Kegan Paul.

11

Integrations with Other Therapies

Role dynamics is a theoretical foundation I have devised not only for psychodrama but also for a more general eclectic approach to psychotherapy. It explains why many kinds of treatment are appropriate: because human nature is so multidimensional. Similarly, our understanding of a problem can have many facets, so concepts derived from different theories can illuminate different aspects of a patient's situation in greater detail. For example, a woman in midlife crisis may have elements of her case that can be best described in terms of family dynamics; other elements, in terms of defense mechanisms; yet others, in terms of communication styles or object relations theory. There may be Jungian themes related to the patient's growing capacity to utilize a healthy internalized image of a woman, Adlerian themes regarding her ways of dealing with a perceived sense of powerlessness, and Freudian themes regarding her associations with members of the opposite sex. Different cases might require techniques or principles derived from William Glasser's reality therapy, Victor Frankl's logotherapy, or

Carl Rogers's client-centered therapy. Each approach addresses different roles in the patient's life. With the use of role dynamics as an overall approach, the individualization of the problem in each case can allow for a more flexible treatment.

Role dynamics attempts to gain a broad perspective regarding the major roles in a person's life and to identify those that are problematical. Recognizing the areas of strength explicitly has several advantages: It raises the patient's self-esteem and helps make the skills associated with the areas of strength available for application in roles that are more conflicted. Another way of thinking about this is that, in addition to approaches that help patients to be rid of sources of extrinsic or intrinsic stress, there are also methods that help them rediscover their positive resources. Cultivating healthy aspects of the personality is as essential to a program of comprehensive treatment as the focused attempt to work out specific emotional conflicts. Such an approach fosters the process of *empowerment* (Blatner, 1987). In other words, role dynamics recognizes that a disorder may be due to the lack of healthy compensatory skills as much as to being simply a reaction to a group of stresses.

Role dynamics is more of a clinical theoretical approach than an academically precise one. It acknowledges the complexity of human nature and social interaction. Roles tend to resist neat definitions and tidy categorizations; they shift, operating on several levels simultaneously and at times paradoxically. It is this very fluidity that allows the therapeutic process its potential for constructive change. Thus, the requirement that a theory be able to explain completely everything about a person's personality is relinquished; it suffices to use the concepts in a practical fashion. Indeed, the relevance or validity of having a perfectly or completely describable phenomenon has increasingly been questioned (Keeny, 1983).

The following clever (and well-known) little story will help me illustrate a relevant issue. There were several blind men in India who encountered an elephant. Each one described the elephant in terms of the part he could feel. Touching the ear, one said, "An elephant is like a fan." Feeling the tail, another said, "An elephant is like a rope." Encountering a leg, a third one said, "The elephant is like a trunk of a tree," and so forth. In the story, they foolishly argued about which one was describing the essence of the beast. Of course, if they had pooled their perceptions, each one admitting that he was perceiving only a part, perhaps their approach could have resulted in wisdom. The psyche can be a bit like the elephant, with theorists saying, "It is like . . ." Role dynamics offers a way to bring the various perceptions together in the service of greater understanding.

People have many facets; it is unnecessary and demeaning to reduce their behavior to "basic" motives or dynamisms. By naming and redefining the relevant roles in a given situation, we have an analytic vehicle for working with our identities and interactions. The seemingly competing theories in psychology can be viewed as describing different dynamics of the same phenomenon. More specifically, I propose it is entirely possible to describe a person's dynamics of functioning in terms of a number of different theories. Each could be seen as being relevant to certain major roles or role components.

Integrating the various dimensions of life is an ongoing process. People achieve a kind of healing through becoming more whole to the extent that they can integrate mind and body, fantasy and reality, desires and actualizations, self and social group, and self and the cosmos (philosophically or spiritually). (The words *wholeness, healing, holism,* and *holy* are all significantly related in essence, as well as in their common root in the ancient Greek language.) In this sense, role dynamics is an intrinsically holistic theory (Staude, 1981). We have roles that relate to the future and others to the past; roles that involve imagination and others that utilize cold logic; roles that focus on basic sensations and others that immerse us in spiritual experience. All of the dualities and paradoxes of human nature are acknowledged.

RAPPROCHEMENT WITH PSYCHOANALYSIS

In 1959 Moreno wrote about a possible rapprochement between psychoanalysis and psychodrama, suggesting primarily that the action methods might complement psychodynamic theory (p. 97). Of course, completely orthodox followers of Freud might balk at this, but the vast majority of practitioners in psychoanalysis are participating in a continuing process of self-criticism and evolution. Thus it is worthwhile to consider some of the essential principles that I think both psychodynamic psychotherapy and the modern practice of psychodrama (which also has been evolving) might have in common:

1. Basic motivations seek expression and gratification; if these

needs are frustrated, they will be expressed in distorted ways.
2. Many psychological operations and experiences occur out of
ordinary awareness.
3. It is possible to expand consciousness to include such
dimensions.
4. It is useful and often necessary to access beliefs or behaviors
that are subconscious in order to reevaluate them and to make
new decisions. This process of reworking old memories and
present habits of mind or behavior is an important form of
psychological healing.
5. Attention must be given to motives that resist this exploratory process, and techniques as well as the personality of the
helper must be refined so as to encourage the patient to take
the risks that are part of experiential learning.
6. Attention must also be given to the process of transference,
or any other distortions of the helping relationship, to opti-
mize the effectiveness of the treatment alliance and to use the
insights about the interactional patterns as clues to more generalized modes of belief and behavior.

I have seen these concepts applied repeatedly in the hands of
competent psychodramatists (who are also professionally trained
and psychodynamically oriented psychotherapists). The use of a
broader range of methods offers a number of advantages in bypass-
ing some of the problems implicit in a purely dyadic, one-to-one
therapy. For example, the use of a third person, a trained
co-therapist who is clearly present to act as an auxiliary by playing
the role of a nurturing parent, can help the patient have a
"corrective emotional experience." The role of a confronting significant other is also often more effective if played by someone
other than the therapist. Blanck and Blanck (1979) noted that the
therapist should be a catalyst, in the sense of being a necessary presence without participating in the action. To this I would add that
having someone else participate could faciiitate the process of therapy even more.

Since Moreno made his suggestion in 1959, family therapy,
group therapy, and other expansions and modifications of technique have become far more accepted. Expanding the therapeutic
repertoire even further might be an idea whose time has come. An
expanded theory and methodology of therapy is inevitable because
the trends toward integration in the field continue to progress.

For example, a recently fashionable group of theorists in psychoanalysis, following the lead of Heinz Kohut, have begun to emphasize the concept of the sense of self in psychoanalysis and the need for empathy on the therapist's part as important components for developing a healthier self-image. Of course, psychodrama offers a powerful modality for amplifying these processes because enactment and play, involving as they do so many aspects of the personality, develop the sense of self in patients far more than does mere verbal dialogue. The empowerment provided by the patients' activity itself must never be underestimated. In psychodrama, empathy is provided more effectively because, first, more than one person witnesses the self-disclosure; second, the avenues of self-disclosure are richer and more likely to circumvent defenses; and third, by responding " in role," there is a degree of mirroring.

A further word about empathy: The technique of doubling can provide more empathy than more conventional interpretations can. First, it does not put the patient on the spot. Instead of being told by an authority, "You feel . . ," the phrasing is more indirect: "If I were in your situation, I might feel . . ." The patient is then invited to correct this amplification. Doubling is presented within what Carl Rogers called the self-system, and the words used are more natural and less psychologized. Using role dynamics, the therapist or auxiliary can more accurately focus on one aspect of the patient's experience at a time, rather than trying to make global inferences about the patient's general affect. Finally, the power of more than one person in providing supportive feedback should be recognized as being qualitatively as well as quantitatively different from when empathy is provided by a single therapist. This is because the dyadic situation is too vulnerable to the tranferential processes of projection and devaluing, and so reassurances are not registered as being quite so "real."

The concept of self, as Moreno suggests, may well be significantly developed in terms of the roles one learns to play. It is an interpersonal process, requiring some degree of validation before it can be consolidated in the psyche. It is also a developmental process, reflecting an ever-widening expansion of identifications. Beginning with the child in relation to its body, it rapidly involves primary caregivers in the reciprocal experience of belonging. In the early months of life, the feeling of effectiveness as an active agent begins, and the self comes to be associated with its own participatory processes (Stern, 1985). By the middle of the first year of life, the child knows that it has the capacity to give as well as to receive. (It is vitally important in any adequate psychology to note that children desire to give and to be useful to others as much as to get and to gratify needs.)

This sense of self continues to expand beyond the mother–child dyad to include the pleasures of vicarious experience. There are also pleasures and a growing sense of self that come with the paradoxical release of desire and identification, with letting go of needs, and with joining with the wholeness in nature. These precursors of spiritual sensitivity and what in later adulthood serve as the foundations of wisdom are also part of the growing sense of self. The paradox is that, as the psyche matures, the earlier requirements for the sense of self dissolve; and more complex and less egocentric ideas and experiences come to serve as sources of satisfaction and security.

The theory of role dynamics can work with the frequently observed phenomenon of patients being more integrated in some facets of their personalities and more immature in others. Thinking in terms of roles, the strengths in one area can be used as a source of imagery and thus become an aid to the development of the less skillful role.

ROLE REVERSAL AND OBJECT RELATIONS THEORY

An interesting example of the use of a role dynamics orientation is evident in reframing some traditional psychoanalytic concepts in order to integrate them with psychodramatic methods to make the psychotherapy more effective. One of the more progressive forms of psychoanalytic thought is the general school of object relations theory, developed by Fairbairn, Federn, Guntrip, and Winnicott in England in the 1950s (Greenberg & Mitchell, 1983). It was influenced by the work of Melanie Klein, and it has correspondences to the work of Harry Stack Sullivan. In essence, the central dynamic is conceptualized not as an individual reacting to outside forces but rather as the person in relation to other people, which often becomes an internalized process. Even the more recent and acclaimed work on the theories of the self by Kohut, Jacobson, and others contains interactional components.

One problem with object relations theory is that the words used give a misleading impression. One therapist told me that the word *object* suggests a kind of lumpy, potato-like contaminant floating about in the soup of the mind. I find this amusing and á propos because the "objects" in the theoretical view are defined as psychological representations of the people who were meaningful earlier in life. However, these representations are not static and left over from the past but rather are continuously being created, like the figures in a dream. Thus it would be better to think of object relations as little dramas created in the mind. These are the "private fictions" that Adler speaks of, but they are more than simple cognitive sets or attitudes. Rather, they are subconscious mini-dramas, interactions in which the person plays both roles: The other figure's behavior often embodies either the hoped-for fulfillments of wishes or the feared and hostile positions that justify familiar power trips on the part of the creator of these fantasies. The dynamism of internalized experience, memories, anticipated repeated traumatic events, symbolic reactions (e.g., "If they do that, I'll show them!") are all part of this complex psychodramatic "inner truth" (Watkins, 1986, pp. 22–28).

The advantage of reframing object relations theory in more dynamic terms is that it leads to the following implication: One way to correct these private fictions is to play them out in a context in which social validation can allow for at least symbolic fulfillment, followed by an opportunity to correct perceptions and resolve conflicts. Role reversal, when done consciously, allows for the workings of spontaneity, the integration of reality testing, and the possibility of the influence of high ideals on the object relationship. Role reversal also expands the patient's perspective beyond the limits of subjectivity. More than any other method in psychotherapy, this helps develop a more mature capacity for "object constancy," the term used in psychoanalysis to describe a more balanced view of the reality of significant others.

This active handling of the theoretical construct of object relations is also in harmony with G. H. Mead's (1934) concept of the "generalized other (i.e., the "they"—"Do they find me attractive: Do they like me? Do they care about my pain?"). This hypothesis describes not a thing called "they" but an active process whereby the person is subconsciously creating the role of a generalized "other person." If there is a tendency to play subtle minidramas in a habitual, stereotyped fashion, it can be channeled into explicit portrayal. Psychodrama is perfect for this. The sources of repetition compulsions may be clarified so that new decisions and strategies can be created and practiced.

I propose we are role-reversing all the time in our minds in a kind of ongoing process for maintaining a sense of social bonding.

There is some resistance to exposing these internalized relationships to the light of explicit consciousness. A range of defense mechanisms symbolically gratify and maintain magical forms of thought by offering pleasant or at least adaptive illusions. It takes a good deal of courage and the support of others to dare to explore alternatives to the problems of personal development in relationships.

INTEGRATIONS WITH OTHER APPROACHES

Cognitive therapies utilize an action-oriented approach that includes role playing. These schools of thought are receiving widespread attention as being psychodynamic, relatively brief, and, according to some highly publicized research, fairly effective (Beck & Greenberg, 1979).

Behavior therapies include the action techniques of rehearsal, modeling, and feedback as part of their basic repertoire. Imagery is also used as an adjunct by Cautela, Salter, Wolpe, and others.

Gestalt therapy has already integrated a number of essential principles of psychodrama. Fritz Perls emigrated from South Africa around 1947 and attended a number of Moreno's sessions, integrating Moreno's role-taking techniques, especially the technique of the empty chair, with his own existential and psychodynamic ideas (Perls, 1973). Exchanges of techniques and principles continue, and the methods are quite compatible. Psychodrama, however, has a greater capacity to be used with approaches.

The creative arts in therapy are naturally allied with applications of psychodrama (McNiff, 1981). Art, music, dance and movement, poetry, and drama approaches have all been used with psychodramatic methods. One approach may function as a warmup or for working through the feelings brought up by the use of another (Feder & Feder, 1981; Robbins, 1980).

Play therapy, although traditionally confined to childhood, has applications in modified form with teenagers and adults. The methods of play therapy integrate more actional approaches (Jernberg, 1979). If they help with children, then, considering the growing recognition that many patients need to work with nonverbal modalities to fully express their feelings, elements of play therapy could be integrated with psychodramatic methods in a comprehensive treatment program with adults also (Tooley, 1973). Furthermore, psychodramatic methods have a potential for enriching the repertoire of the play therapist by offering a variety of scenarios and ways for exploring scenes.

The body therapies, including the works of F. M. Alexander, Ida Rolf, Moshe Feldenkrais, Milton Trager, and especially Alexander Lowen's bioenergetic analysis are often effective approaches for mobilizing affects and memories (Geller, 1978). Lowen's work is an offshoot of Wilhelm Reich's theories of "body armoring," noting the way patients insulate themselves from feelings of vulnerability and other impulses through chronic patterns of muscle tension. Pesso's psychomotor therapy (1969) is also an interesting contribution in this area. In practice, this approach is not infrequently used, along with psychodrama, to add some of the cognitive dimensions to the therapy.

Imagination therapies, such as those proposed by Leuner, Ahsen, Shorr, and others, all contain elements that complement psychodrama and, in turn, could be enriched by the inclusion of psychodramatic techniques such as asides, role portrayal, and role reversal. These approaches also make bridges between cognitive therapies, expressive therapies, and hypnotherapies (Shorr, 1974). The visualization processes associated with biofeedback training can also include psychodramatic devices such as the surplus-reality techniques of future projection or redoing the past in a more congenial fashion.

Hypnotherapy was combined with psychodrama early in its development. Indeed, psychodramatic enactment often generates a mild to moderate level of trance in the protagonist and other participants. Some of the more recent techniques in the rapidly growing field of hypnotherapy [and its associated approach of neurolinguistic programming (NLP)] include psychodramatic principles such as having parts of the self dialogue with each other and with a newly suggested synthesizing self.

Adlerian therapy (Individual psychology) was felt by Rudolf Dreikurs to be a natural complement to psychodrama; he arranged for an associate, Adaline Starr (1973), to attend Moreno's academy and develop this line of collaboration. Since then, psychodrama has been a regular part of the curriculum at the Alfred Adler Institute in Chicago and has been adapted as a integrated form by Shoobs, O'Connell, and others.

Jungian therapy (Analytical psychology) also offers opportunities for the integration of psychodramatic methods. Watkins (1986) describes a rich usage of imaginal dialogue for working with archetypal images, and it is but a small step to acting them out. James Hillman's modification and extension of Jungian thought, which he calls archetypal psychology, is similarly a potential candidate for using actional techniques. Such techniques can function to increase the vividness of the imagination, which Hillman (1983) considers the essence of soul-making and the true goal of his approach to psychotherapy(pp. 26–27, 44).

Family therapy has utilized a variety of active and directive approaches. It is a natural context for applying psychodramatic techniques, especially those of the aside, behind-the-back, role reversal, and the double. (Perrott, 1986).

Group therapy has been using action techniques more frequently in the last few decades, and other psychodramatic methods could be easily included. Of course, combining an interactive group approach with more complex psychodrama generates one of the most powerful modes of healing I know.

Miscellaneous eclectic therapies such as Phillips's conflict resolution therapy, Pederson's triadic counseling, Kelly's personal construct therapy, O'Connell's natural high therapy, Watkins's ego state therapy, Rosen's direct analysis, Lazarus's multimodal therapy, Janov's primal therapy, Urban's integrative therapy, and Shutz's holistic therapy all contain Morenean actional and role-playing elements (Corsini, 1981; Grayson & Loew, 1978).

In summary, I have presented a theoretical system that can function as an adequate intellectual foundation for psychodrama and other therapies, especially emphasizing its usefulness as a workable tool for clinical practice. I know of no other theory that can encompass the many varieties of human experience. I propose that role dynamics should be considered seriously as a viable option for an integrative system of psychosocial thought.

REFERENCES

Beck, Aaron T., & Greenberg, Ruth L. (!979). Brief cognitive therapies. *Psychiatric Clinics of North America, 2*(1), 23–37.

Blanck, Gertrude, & Blanck, Rubin. (1979). *Ego psychology—II.* New York: Columbia University Press.

Blatner, Adam. (1987). Preface. In Morris R. Morrison (Ed.), *Poetry as therapy.* New York: Human Sciences Press.

Corsini, Raymond J. (Ed.). *Handbook of innovative therapies.* New York: Wiley/Interscience.

Feder, Elaine, & Feder, Bernard. (1981). *The expressive arts therapies.* Englewood Cliffs, NJ: Prentice-Hall.

Geller, Jesse D. (1978). The body, expressive movement, and physical contact. In Jerome L. Singer & Kenneth S. Pope (Eds.), *The power of human imagination: New methods in psychotherapy* (pp. 347–378). New York: Plenum.

Grayson, Henry H., & Loew, Clemens. (Eds.). (1987). *Changing approaches to the psychotherapies*. New York: Spectrum/Halstead.

Greenberg, Jay R., & Stephen A. Mitchell. (1983). *Object relations in psychoanalytic theory*. Cambridge, MA: Harvard University Press.

Hillman, James. (1983). *Archetypal psychology; A brief account*. Dallas, TX: Spring Publications.

Jernberg, Ann M. (1979). *Theraplay*. San Francisco: Jossey-Bass.

Keeny, Bradford P. (1983). *Aesthetics of change*. New York: Guilford.

McNiff, Shaun. (1981). *The arts and psychotherapy*. Springfield, IL: Charles C. Thomas.

Mead, George H. (1934). *Mind, self, and society*. Chicago: University of Chicago Press.

Moreno, J. L. (1959). *Psychodrama* (Vol. 2). Beacon, NY: Beacon House.

Perls, Fritz. (1973). Shuttling, psychodrama, and confusion. *The Gestalt approach*. Palo Alto, CA: Science and Behavior Books.

Perrott, Louis A. (1986). Using psychodramatic techniques in structural family therapy. *Contemporary Family Therapy, 8* (4), 279–290.

Pesso, Albert. (1969). *Movement in psychotherapy*. New York: New York University Press.

Robbins, Arthur. (1980). *Expressive therapy*. New York; Human Sciences Press.

Shorr, Joseph E. (19740. *Psychotherapy through imagery*. New York: Intercontinental Medical Book Corp.

Starr, Adaline. (1973). Sociometry of the family. In Harold H. Mosak (Ed.), *Alfred Adler: His influence on psychology today* (pp. 95–105). Park Ridge, NJ: Noyes Press.

Staude, John-Raphael. (1981). *The adult development of C. G. Jung*. Boston: Routledge and Kegan Paul.

Stern, Daniel. (1985). *The interpersonal world of the infant*. New York: Basic Books.

Tooley, Kay. (1973). Playing it right. *Journal of the American Academy of Child Psychiatry, 12*(4), 615–631.

Watkins, Mary. (1986). *Invisible guests: The development of imaginal dialogue*. Hillsdale, NJ: Erlbaum/The Analytic Press.

PART IV
Social Foundations

12

Psychodrama and the Interpersonal Field

Psychodrama, its theoretical basis of role dynamics, and its associated approaches of sociodrama and sociometry offer a relatively unique repertoire of resources for dealing with the complexities of what I term "the interpersonal field." Others have addressed aspects of this important dimension of human experience (e.g., Eric Berne's method of transactional analysis and the work of communications theorists such as Jay Haley and Gregory Bateson); however, they do not encompass the whole range of phenomena. For example, consider the importance of the following issues when investigating the interpersonal field:

- How do people work out conflicts, distribute tasks or roles in a group, and renegotiate issues in relationships?
- How are some relationships unhealthy even if the individuals involved would be considered healthy in most other situations? Also, how is it that some people who might be considered unhealthy in many contexts can be involved in relatively healthy relationships?

- What are the bases of preference and choice in relationships?
- What is the power of reciprocated feelings, and how are relationships affected by various ways of evoking, communicating, interpreting, and responding to such feelings?
- How can issues of expectations, temperamental differences, and different values, life-styles, or interests be addressed more explicitly?
- How can problems due to different styles of verbal and nonverbal communications and problem solving be diagnosed and corrected?

These issues, which will be discussed briefly in the following chapters, are often central to human experience. They reflect neither the psychodynamics of the individual nor the dynamics of a large group; they are phenomena related to the interpersonal field. Although Harry Stack Sullivan attempted to extend psychoanalytic thinking to include interpersonal dynamics, as has the more currently popular object relations school of psychoanalysis, I think these efforts have been handicapped by a methodology that worked with the person alone in psychotherapy. [Moreno (1953), p. lx, claims to have used the term "interpersonal" before it was used by Sullivan.] On the other hand, sociologists and social psychologists generally address interactions in a descriptive fashion that lacks any methodology for dealing with the misunderstandings and conflicts in relationships. Also, they often work on a more general psychological level that does not account for the richness of individual differences.

The interpersonal field is certainly addressed by family systems theorists, but here, too, the dimension is distorted by the overly intimate and longstanding nature of the family. However, the Morenean approach can also include relationships such as friends, clubs, churches, classmates, co-workers, and so on. Moreover, the Morenean approach offers methods that the people involved can use to evaluate and correct problems as they arise, such as the techniques of role reversal, multiple parts of self, the mirror, and replay.

The interpersonal field represents a level of human experience between the intrapsychic and the sociocultural dimensions. For example, understanding a child's difficulties at school may include the intrapsychic level, such as feelings and behaviors carried over from home; a sociocultural level, such as having to cope with a competitive system overly oriented to verbal skills; and an interpersonal level, such as relationships with the other children in class. A psychotherapy that addresses only one or two of these levels leaves out other major considerations.

Each level of complexity requires its own methods for diagnosing and treating problems. In this sense, an analogy may be drawn to understanding biological processes, where there are also three levels: chemical/molecular, cellular, and organ (gross anatomical), each of which is analyzed by different kinds of instruments and changed by different kinds of treatments. Thus, dysfunctions on a chemical level usually cannot be treated by surgery, whereas defects on the organ level–blockages, tears, or wrong connections–usually cannot be treated just with medicines. As for the middle level, the cellular, it should be noted that instruments for knowing about this dimension were available for more than a century before they were used in practical ways by most physicians–and that occurred only about 100 years ago. (There is an analogy to be drawn with the relatively recent awareness of the potential of sociometry and related methods for dealing with the interpersonal realm, which have yet to be applied on a widespread basis.) Since doctors have become aware of the cellular level of physiology, a variety of methods aimed at that level have evolved (e.g., radiation, heat, transfusions). In a similar fashion, when psychotherapists and sociotherapists become aware of the interpersonal field, they may be able to use sociodramatic and psychodramatic methods for working out the problems in this sphere. Of course, these approaches can be used in association with (and as complements to) work on the levels of individual psychodynamics and/or changing the social system.

TELE: THE INTERPERSONAL CONDITION

People are often attracted to or repelled by each other, and the intangible "force" or "connection" or "condition" (this last term perhaps is the most accurate) that describes this dynamic is what Moreno termed "tele." It represents the sense of preference in all of its permutations, and so one definition of tele is that which is measured by sociometry. Tele is a generic term for all of the factors that account for preferences between people. The concept need not be excessively abstract. Think of those you prefer or like in certain ways: Those are people with whom you have positive tele. There are others who evoke a sense of discomfort or repulsion, and with them you have negative tele. Some people you know are relevant in your life, but your feelings are neutral; this is called neutral tele. Others around you are not relevant to your interests, and with them you are indifferent.

Tele is a useful word because there is no other term I can think of that functions as a general category for the variety of interpersonal reactions. Rapport is only one form of tele, as is transference. Attraction does not include the other types—repulsion, neutral, and so on. Furthermore, a preference may be based on factors other than attraction, such as competence. For example, you may prefer certain medical specialists for their reputations as skillful technicians, whereas for other specialists the factor of personal rapport would be more important.

Moreno made a special point of differentiating tele from transference. In some psychoanalytically oriented circles, any reaction of a patient toward a therapist has come to be called transference—which more meticulous analysts have noted as an error. Technically, transference is always a distortion, a carrying over into the therapeutic relationship of expectations or reaction patterns learned in earlier significant relationships. However, there are many reactions of patients in therapy that are based on the reality of the therapist's verbal or nonverbal behavior (Greenson & Wexler, 1969). These should be considered aspects of tele because most forms of tele are based on relatively realistic factors.

However, it must be noted that transferential expectations, projections, and other forms of irrational thinking are pervasive in relationships, and part of the challenge of dynamic psychotherapy in the last century has been to rectify the disturbances caused by these distortions. For example, a person may like or dislike others for reasons that are unexamined and unrealistic. A man may be attracted to women because of the sexual stereotypes of desirability presented in the mass media, rather than having any sense of more enduring sources for compatibility. With such a set of criteria, he may be unable to notice the type of women who might find him attractive.

One of the values of the concept of tele is that it helps us to become more sensitive to the reasons we feel some preferences, whether they be attractions or repulsions. This awareness then makes it possible to discuss, negotiate, and find creative alternatives regarding areas of conflict. Of course, the various methods associated with sociometry and psychodrama are most helpful in this task.

One of the most important factors that influences tele is the presence or absence of reciprocity (this will be discussed below). Some other reasons people tend to prefer or reject others include the following variables:

temperamental similarities	temperamental differences
regional background	cultural background
ability or experience	life-style, values
exotic differences	smell, sound of voice
familiarity	physical proximity
a worthy competitor	an easy "mark" or "win"
level of vitality	common interests
role complementarity:	attractiveness:
leader/follower	physical, sexual,
active/passive	intellectual, social,
helper/helpee	spiritual, playful,
talker/listener	emotional, artistic

And most importantly: reciprocity.

The relevance of any of these factors, or others you may think of, shifts with role and context. In a given situation, the naming of the specific issues involved is necessary if we are to truly understand the interaction. Indeed, the clarification and expression of the reasons for an interpersonal preference, whether aimed at an individual or a group, can function as a source of relevant material in psychotherapy. This interpersonal dimension is based on roles, so whom one chooses as a tennis partner may differ from whom one chooses as a working partner. People will tend to choose a church or club to some extent on the sense of the group being "our kind of people." Thus, the telic structure in a person's life varies with the criteria being used.

The criterion by which a preference is exercised could be either sociotelic, referring to a shared goal or common interest, or psychetelic, referring to personal qualities or rapport that exist aside from any utilitarian reason. Sociotelic criteria might be more operative in a group in a church or in the community that meets because of a special area of concern; psychetelic criteria would be operating in the natural subgroupings or cliques that get together for coffee, invite each other to parties, or play outside at recess.

Becoming aware of the reasons for tele helps to counter tendencies to overidealize or generally devalue by noting that a person may be appreciated in some roles while not being particularly spe-

cial in others. This also suggests that people should be free to renegotiate their roles in groups so that they are not subtly compelled
to function in a way that is least likely for them to be enjoyed.
Explorations of such themes could be useful in ongoing group
therapy or within a therapeutic community.

RECIPROCITY

Reciprocity refers to the phenomenon in which a feeling is
returned in kind. If one likes another, it tends to evoke similar feelings in return. Similarly, disliking is often reciprocated. Often,
there is no obvious reason, and blame need not be placed on either
participant. Tele reactions are often reciprocated, but not necessarily. Mixed tele consists of interactions in which one person prefers
another, but in turn is not preferred by the other (or the other is
indifferent or neutral toward the person). Such interactions may
serve as useful sources for reexamination of the criteria for choice
in the situation.

The theme of reciprocity is very useful in psychotherapy because
it deals with the complexity of interpersonal relationships. Rather
than being a one-way or even two-way process, interactions are
viewed as involving a sequence of many communications and interpretations. Thus, interactions can become dysfunctional if either
party:

- sends confusing messages, whether they include incongruent
  nonverbal signals or vague, circumstantial, or evasive verbal
  communications.
- indicates insufficient response.
- misinterprets the others' communications.
- is unwilling to or does not know how to check out the validity
  of an interpretation.
- signals that the process of communication is not an acceptable
  subject for comment.
- communicates negative expectations.
- is insensitive to nonverbal cues or even clear statements.

A sense of mutuality is developed when the participants in a relationship can communicate an openness to offering or receiving
attention, interest, respect, help, or support. Mutuality also
increases as people can reciprocally indicate a willingness to exert

an equal amount of effort toward a shared goal. Discussion of these themes in therapy and education offers foundations for building skills in more effective communications. When people have a greater sense of mastery through knowing a variety of mature techniques for getting attention or making boundaries, they are less likely to regress to the use of manipulations.

Another reason the concept of reciprocity is useful is that it offers a powerful tool for exploring the phenomena of transference, projection, and other distortions of the interpersonal field. By discussing the general ideas of tele, preferences, reciprocity, and the like, patients are given a general framework, a simple language, along with an expectation or norm of examining the accuracy and motivations in interpersonal relationships.

LIKING AND BEING LIKED

An important aspect of interpersonal psychodynamics is the experience of feeling liked. It is qualitatively different from feeling tolerated or accepted, which implies a rather neutral process. To be liked suggests that one feels somewhat enjoyable to others, certainly enough so that occasional minor lapses in appropriate behavior will be forgiven or even overlooked. More, it offers a positive sense of validation, a source of self-esteem, and a feeling of having been socially useful.

It is a sensitive issue because inquiry regarding one's likability can easily be met with a negative answer. In terms of tele, most people have relatively neutral or indifferent tele with most others. That is, if they were to ask a broad section of all those who know them on sight, and if the responses were honest, they would discover that they were not actively liked very much. The problem of knowing about all of that neutral and indifferent tele is that most people do not know what to do with the information. How much does one need to be liked in order to be successful? Is a person all right, normal, or secure enough to be liked by only a relatively small number of people?

Being liked is an excellent theme for psychotherapy because it surfaces these and many other issues:

- How does one go about being liked? Is it the same as being popular? By whom is it necessary to be liked in order to make other friends?

- What should people do if it becomes apparent that they are not in a group of people who like them? Can the reasons be discovered? Can a negative reputation be repaired? Are there any other groups that might be more congenial?
- What are the requirements for basic likability? How much does one have to fulfill the expectations or needs of others in order to achieve likability? Can one be liked even if there are some handicaps?

Some of these concerns are addressed in Chapter 13. Others may serve as sources for discussion in individual or group therapy. Helping patients to develop strategies for building socially enjoyable relationships involves a number of components.

One problem in this area is that the psychodynamic therapies have arisen out of work with hysterical patients, usually young women, for whom the key issue was not what they could learn but whether they could be liked by the therapist. Manipulations to gain approval, admiration, or sexual interest served as common resistances to analytic work, which was also complicated by the tradition of working in a one-to-one and confidential context, which in its very format tended to promote intense transferential reactions. Under such conditions, encouraging therapists to cultivate ways of liking their patients seemed counterproductive.

It is important to diagnose the subtle dynamic of the patient's wanting to substitute narcissistic gratification for real work. (I find the psychoeducational approach helpful in keeping the task of developing skills foremost.) However, in most cases building an active treatment alliance can safely include a measure of enjoyment, and in turn this promotes a more balanced willingness to explore the more painful facets of life (Blatner & Blatner, 1987).

It may well be that therapists themselves are often more vulnerable to concerns about their own likability than is generally recognized. These issues are not easily dealt with in individual psychotherapy or in a training analysis. Furthermore, the role of the therapist often serves as a protective buffer to the challenge of mutuality in relationships. Another reason the themes of likability may be avoided is that few people are sufficiently acquainted with methods for diagnosing or correcting problems in the interpersonal field.

OUR SOCIAL BEING-NESS

Appreciating the extent of our immersion in a social context is not only a sociological observation but also an esthetic and philosophical contemplation. Trigant Burrow, an early psychoanalyst, made this perspective a key element in his little-known (but worth rediscovering) writings (Burrow, 1964). He felt that many aspects of psychodynamics should be recognized as expressing our relative alienation from a more integrated existence. Wallach and Wallach (1983) also explore the tendencies of modern dynamic psychology to overemphasize the individualistic aspects of experience. In contrast, a psychology such as the type presented in this book is more likely to encourage a shift away from egocentricity and toward what Adler called "social interest" or "fellow feeling" (Crandall, 1981).

It is important to differentiate individuation from individualism. The former refers to the bringing forth of the unique potentials inherent in each person, and it can happen—indeed, happens most fully—in a culture that is healthily socially integrated and prizes cooperative action. Individualism, the protective valuing of individual prerogatives even at a major cost to others, is a social doctrine that promotes selfishness and egocentricity. We see the cultural belief in individualism reflected in the recent phenomenon of winning being valued more than fairness in sports (Montagu, 1982).

The sciences also express the collective world view. I suspect many psychologies are biased toward individualistic concerns because they are actually expressing an unconscious repression of our collective nature. Ernest Becker (1973) has touched on this theme, but he did not go far enough, in my opinion. The individualistic bias tends to lead to a view that our interconnectedness is an illusion; however, it might be argued even more cogently that it is individualism that is the illusion and that our true human nature is really more collective than we realize. The belief in our separateness is reinforced by the kinds of psychodynamics described by Alfred Adler in his system of individual psychology. When he points out the healing alternative of the feeling of social interest, he begins to partake of what Jung referred to in his concept of the collective unconscious. The resistance to opening to the depth of our common humanity reflects an almost archetypal fear of loss of identity or autonomy within the group.

The sweep of history reflects a theme of the emergence of the individual from the undifferentiated collective, and there has been some value in this, in that more creativity has been liberated. However, we now have methods (such as sociometry and sociodrama) that can transform groups into instruments for enhancing rather than diminishing individuality (Fink, 1963). Thus, the time has come to bring a new synthesis to the previous dialectical tension between the individual and the group.

In summary, the interpersonal field is a multidimensional arena of human experience that should be recognized as a level of psychosocial organization distinct from (and between) those of intrapsychic dynamics and sociological, or group, dynamics. It involves such phenomena as the variations of interpersonal preferences, reciprocity, liking and being liked, role analysis, and an awareness of our social interdependence.

REFERENCES

Becker, Ernest. (1973). *The denial of death.* New York: The Free Press.

Blatner, Adam, & Blatner, Allee. (1987). *The art of play: An adult's guide to reclaiming imagination and spontaneity.* New York: Human Sciences Press.

Burrow, Trigant. (1964). *Preconscious foundations of human experience* (Ed. by William E. Galt). New York: Basic Books.

Crandall, James E. (1981). *The theory and measurement of social interest.* New York: Columbia University Press.

Fink, Abel K. (1963). The democratic essence of psychodrama. *Group Psychotherapy, 16*(3), 156–160.

Greenson, Ralph R., & Wexler, Milton. (1969). The non-transference relationship in the psychoanalytic situation. *International Journal of Psycho-Analysis, 50,* 27–40

Montagu, Ashley. (1982). The decay of sport values. In J. Partington, T. Orlick, & S. S. Salmela (Eds.), *Sport in perspective* (pp. 170–176). Ottawa: Sport in Perspective.

Wallach, Michael A., & Wallach, Lise. (1983). *Psychology's sanction for selfishness: The error of egoism in theory and therapy.* San Francisco: W. H. Freeman.

13

The Implications of Sociometry

The sociopsychological aspect of psychodrama is elaborated by Moreno in his theory of sociometry, an approach that represents not only a group of methods but, more importantly, a philosophy of collective and applied research. Moreno's vision is simply that people should participate actively in the examination and restructuring of their own group dynamics. Sociometry is a manifestation of the spirit of democracy, a humanistic approach in which people are recognized as being creatively involved in their sociological process and should not be thought of as mere organisms on whom scientists do research (Kosemihal, 1959). In this chapter, rather than explicating the technical aspects of sociometry, I will discuss some general theoretical concepts that complement the literature in the field.

Sociometry has been a relatively obscure aspect of Moreno's work, although he considered it to be as important as psychodrama. Because his interest was in promoting the health of groups, organizations, and society as a whole, he wanted to develop meth-

ods for clarifying the dynamics and working out the problems that
are so prevalent on these more complex levels. Indeed, he even
envisioned a form of therapist, a sociatrist, who would use sociometry and sociodrama for dealing with intergroup problems, just
as psychodrama can help with interpersonal conflicts. This chapter
will discuss some of the reasons for Moreno's belief in sociometry,
especially in terms of the dimensions of interpersonal relations that
are highlighted by the method.

To begin with, it must be noted that sociometry has two levels
of reference. It describes a relatively specific method for discovering the hidden structure of relationships in groups and, in a more
general sense, a broader approach to group dynamics and social
psychology. This two-level definition is similar to the nature of
psychoanalysis, which also may be thought of both as a specific
technique and a much wider field of activity.

A BRIEF DESCRIPTION OF SOCIOMETRIC METHODS

As a method, sociometry serves to give people in a group feedback
as to their collective patterns of interpersonal preferences. By facilitating systematic disclosure, sociometry opens the way for the
group to deal directly with its dynamics, to work out conflicts,
shift group norms or structures, and/or renegotiate roles to maxi-
mize inclusion and group cohesion.

The specific method of sociometry involves asking members of
a group to express their preferences about which other group
members they would choose to share some activity. Perhaps the
most common use of this approach is the technique of allowing
group members to choose each other for a dyadic structured exercise. Sometimes this is preceded by having the group stand up and
mill around, making eye contact or even greeting each other
nonverbally in a variety of fashions (e.g., "Now back into someone," "Say hello with your eyes closed," "Say hello with your
backs," etc.). The experience of having chosen someone and/or
being chosen in turn is itself a powerful way to develop group
cohesion, and it plants the seeds for future explorations of the bases
for these choices (which will be discussed below).

Another frequent use of a sociometric technique is in helping a
group choose a protagonist: If several people have an issue and
want to work, the director invites the group to listen to the

"candidates" as they describe their issues, and then group members go up and put one hand on the shoulder of the possible protagonist whose issues seem most relevant to each of them. This helps the group make explicit any common themes.

A variation that is aimed more at focusing on individual dynamics is that of having patients in individual or group psychotherapy diagram their social atoms. This serves as a useful component in warming them up to explorations in their interpersonal field. It is applicable in the early stages of diagnosis or evaluation in psychotherapy because patients recognize immediately the relevance of this dimension of experience. Enacting the patient's social network as if it were a "sculptured" diorama is often useful in therapy—the "action sociogram" has been adopted by family therapists in a number of ways. The technique can be expanded by having patients note (or demonstrate) how they think significant others in the family or group might set up the sociogram, and what they think these others think of them. (This brings out perceptions of reciprocity, as described in Chapter 12). In group therapy, other variations, such as the "spectrogram" or modified forms of action sociometry, serve as vehicles for warming up to more specific explorations and sometimes as powerful sources of feedback—for either support or confrontation. All of these variations nevertheless contain the essential idea of helping people to make explicit their preferences and perceptions of others' feelings toward them.

The original and best-known method of sociometry is a paper-and-pencil process, in which participants note the others in the group with whom they would prefer to share a given activity (Hale, 1974, 1985). Ideally, choosing what activity is being asked about also becomes part of the sociometric process. Examples of questions might be as follows: With whom would you like to sit at lunch? Whom would you prefer to have as a laboratory partner? What subgroup do you want to work with while planning a party? The answers may be indicated on paper, perhaps several ranked in order of preference. Negative preferences—those with whom one would rather not work/play in a given situation—may or may not be included in the exercise. The results are collected, tabulated, and diagrammed, and various patterns of functioning can be discovered. Ideally, in Moreno's opinion, this information should be shared with the group so that they can then fulfill the purpose implied by the question—assigning people to tables at lunch, as laboratory partners, and so on. For example, during World War II this method was applied in helping some flying units organize their troops so that people who had good rapport could work together, and it was found to increase overall effectiveness.

In this way, sociometry is a social analog of biofeedback. Elmer Green, one of the pioneers of biofeedback, pointed out that the instrumentation is not the change agent but rather the psychosomatic skills of subtle self-regulation. The machine only functions like a bathroom scale in the process of weight control. So, too, it is not the actual sociometric technique that is the essential idea but rather the commitment to self-disclosure and clear, consensual feedback, followed by an exercise of skills in improving interpersonal relations and group cohesion.

HISTORICAL PERSPECTIVES

The roots of sociometry begin in Moreno's experiences in 1917, when he was assigned as a physician during World War I to care for a community of Italian Tyrolean refugees who were given a camp outside Vienna. His goal was to help in the formation of cooperative subcommunities, based on the preferences of the people themselves rather than any externally generated or arbitrarily determined living arrangements. In the early 1930s, he developed the method further while acting as a consultant at the Hudson School for Girls in New York, and these experiments became the basis for Moreno's most elaborate book, *Who Shall Survive* (1934, 1953b).

Over the next few decades, sociometry became more recognized as one of the earlier approaches to social psychology. It was encouraged by such notables as William A. White, Gardner Murphy, Read Bain, F. Stuart Chapin, and others. One of the most important (and insufficiently recognized) figures in the field of sociometry was Helen Hall Jennings (1950, 1959). In the 1950s and 1960s, the method was utilized primarily in the educational system (Evans, 1962; Gronlund, 1959; Northway, 1967). However, many other applications were noted in the books and journals Moreno published (see Bibliography).

Sociometry and its related approaches of psychodrama and group therapy require a commitment to greater levels of honesty, and attention is given to the actual relationships in the here-and-now. If this begins to sound like the ethos of the encounter group, it is. Moreno's work was in actuality the precursor of that approach, not only in spirit but also in direct historical influence. Several of the people who were later to become founders of the T-group (such as Ronald Lippitt and Leland Bradford), although primarily working with Kurt Lewin, had been in contact with Moreno and were familiar with his methods (Moreno, 1953a). Some of their seminal papers, around the time of the organization of the first T-groups in 1946 and 1947, were published in Moreno's journals (Lippitt, Bradford, & Benne, 1947). In those early experiments, role playing and other structured actional approaches were significant parts of the process. A few years later, the experiments in education and community organizational development became a more popular method of sensitivity training; and a decade later, this approach in a sense fused with the emerging field of humanistic psychology to become the encounter group.

Another branch of the T-group movement was co-opted by the psychoanalytically oriented group dynamics workers in England and then reimplanted in the United States. This so-called Tavistock approach regressed to the use of the passivity of the group leader as a major technique for evoking interpersonal interactions. (The emphasis was, as could be predicted, on the tendencies to work out dependency conflicts and other transferences with the leader, which I think was in fact largely an artifact of the way the groups were run. When there is more structure, participants get down to more self-generated interpersonal issues.)

In the field of sociology, sociometry was one of the first scientific methods, and it has continued to serve as an instrument for research. However, Moreno's intention was for it to be used as far more than an academic exercise (Mendelson, 1977). He wanted what might be called today an applied behavioral science, one that directly helped the people who were being tested. This was not simply a matter of his interests but rather an ethical imperative and also an extension of his existential philosophy. Sociometry was a tool people could use to monitor the state of their own collective functioning, and with this information they could make informed decisions about changing group norms, procedures, and roles. Thus, academic sociology was not asking the relevant questions, in Moreno's opinion. Beyond describing the phenomena of group dynamics, it is important to identify, create, and work out the technical problems involved in attempting to correct "group illnesses." This requires an interdisciplinary approach and, as such, has yet to develop a recognized body of knowledge and a degree of expert status.

Of course, sociometry required more than what was part of the repertoire of skills of the average academician. Few professors of sociology or social psychology are equally trained in group therapy, and such a synthesis of disciplines was necessary for the emergence of what Moreno called sociotherapists or sociatrists. This new field of professionals would have a socially recognized role in diagnosing and treating conflicts within and between groups, neighborhoods, organizations, and even nations, like that of a psychotherapist treating an individual or a family. Certainly, there is room for such a role, because larger collectives exhibit even more dangerous forms of psychopathology and self-deception. The rudimentary state of our knowledge and the presence of collective resistances should not deter us from envisioning and building toward recognition of the validity and methods in such a role.

RESISTANCES TO SOCIOMETRY

Just as there are resistances to exploring the depth of the intrapsychic realm, so also are there individual and collective resistances to exploring the interpersonal field. The questions that are asked in sociometric explorations are significant ones. They evoke fears that self and/or others will be hurt if not chosen. Moreover, the reasons for the choices often tend to reflect deeply meaningful feelings. Indeed, if dreams are the "royal road to the unconscious," as Freud said, then sociometry would be the "jet stream." The bases for preferences regarding work, church, mate, hobby, and style of clothes have many connections to the unconscious life, and furthermore these connections take on more significance than dreams because they are so obviously determining factors in living. Thus, people sense that pursuing these issues could rapidly lead them into levels of self-examination that many would rather avoid.

Another resistance to sociometry is the subconscious yet prevalent feeling that interpersonal relationships are too complex to work out. People experience a mild hopelessness caused by a mixture of factors:

- Suspecting others of what are really their own worst motivations (i.e., projection). They distrust others to the extent they cannot trust themselves to be socially inclusive.
- Denying the reality of interpersonal tension, similar to the way some people deny early signs of medical illness—they hope it will magically go away. They ignore the truth that

problems in the long run will either force themselves to be worked out openly or fester like an abscess, getting worse with time.
- Lacking exposure to constructive alternatives, they cannot imagine there is a better way.

These common psychological forms of self-deception are major contributors to our present unhealthy level of social alienation. Psychodramatic and sociometric methods can be used constructively to address this problem. As people learn to use the skills of group and interpersonal awareness as tools, they may become ready to face knowing who in the group is isolated or rejected and for what reasons, whose perceptions about being liked or disliked are mistaken, which subgroups exist, and what the different roles or criteria are by which one can be recognized. Our present culture is characterized by a number of social changes that require a heightened level of psychological flexibility and creative coping skills. These can be developed through educational group experiences that utilize sociometry and psychodramatic methods.

In other words, the sociometric process demands that a person be willing to make explicit preferences, which, in our culture, generally are enacted in a state of polite evasiveness. It is probable that sociometry has not been more widely recognized or accepted because it is realistically threatening. Very few group leaders feel capable of trying to work out the confusing and hurt feelings that can be generated in the course of such a procedure.

Thus, for a group to be able to benefit from sociometry requires a corresponding capacity to use group dynamics constructively, and the skills involved in both endeavors are rare in our society. The people in a group who will be receptive to sociometry are those who have some confidence that they will be able to make good use of the information generated. Such confidence, in turn, rests on a familiarity with group methods, especially the psychodramatic techniques of role reversal, doubling, and other affirmative approaches to conflict resolution. Even most conventional group therapists do not know these skills and are themselves wary about engaging in open conflict with colleagues.

Sociometry and psychodrama require spontaneity, and spontaneity requires some degree of freedom from anxiety. This means a willingness to change thoughtfully in the face of new information—an existential flexibility and courage that comes from knowing how to access others for support. In short, one major source of resistance to sociometry is the lack of mastery of a range of component skills for working out problems in a positive way. Sociometry is like taking a scalpel to a patient, and if you are not ready to proceed with the process of surgery (the equivalent is psychodrama), then you have inflicted a wound on the person (group members). This is not meant to exclude the use of sociometric techniques to enhance a group's functioning. I am referring to sociometry in its fullest meaning as a diagnostic and catalytic agent.

THERAPEUTIC IMPLICATIONS

Related to this is the power of the implied questions that are raised in the course of sociometric process. For example, really exploring the basis for your choice of vocation, mate, and place to live will evoke a wealth of associations. You can discover more important aspects of your subconscious functioning by pursuing this kind of exercise than in any other specific technique in psychotherapy. The act of choosing is a multidetermined process, involving a wide range of sensitive motivations. Thus, sociometry can be adapted as a technique of psychotherapy because of the intangibles involved in tele, that interpersonal connectedness expressed by the process of making preferences explicit. (A handy definition of tele is that quality in relationships that is measured by sociometry.)

When people consider the implications of their social networks, they become aware of whom they prefer to be with in various activities. This often leads to several discoveries. For example, their range of expectations about social relationships may have become constricted. They may be settling for less than they need to in terms of how others might treat them. Also, becoming aware of their ability to choose alternatives may lead to dissatisfactions with family, neighborhood, subculture, and so on, and these feelings can become mixed with anxiety about temptations to move into the unknown and fears of change. Thus, the process can be socially destabilizing unless it is balanced by a variety of channels for reconstructing social networks, and these channels are not always available.

Reading the professional literature on sociometry generally does not communicate the power of the method, especially when used with teenagers or adults. The apparently simple question, "Whom do you prefer . . ?" inevitably leads to a number of corollaries: "What is the basis for your choice? What are the influences on your choosing?

Might you or others be hurt by not being highly chosen by others?"

One of the potential contributions of sociometry is the idea that people who like each other often work better together than do people who are grouped according to other criteria (such as alphabetical order, height, etc.). Yet in many organizations, friends have been actively separated because such relations were often felt to be distracting. It is entirely possible that more work and learning could have occurred if people with positive reciprocal tele were encouraged to sit together, work on projects together, and in other ways have those informal relationships validated. This dynamic has been extensively confirmed by using sociometric testing in schools, military organizations, and industry.

The lack of validation of sociometric choices in child devlopment leads to a good deal of subtle psychopathology. Without opportunities for natural selection in a variety of roles, it becomes harder to choose one's associates effectively. It is a skill that requires experimentation and practice, just like any other. For example, having to work with others whose pace of action or learning is much faster or slower can reinforce feelings of being different and inadequate. Many people not only have difficulty finding their "own kind of people" to work or play with, they do not even know that these natural connections exist.

Therefore, it would be an important component of preventive mental health for schools, recreational programs, and related institutions to make a point of helping children explore a variety of interests. As it is, there is an overemphasis on competitive athletics or the performance activities. Teachers, administrators, counselors, and parents can begin to promote a sense that young people can be popular in their own natural groups, rather than being allowed to continue to struggle with the present system based on sports, beauty, money, unusual talent, or social competence. An affirmative approach to validating a wide variety of interests—science, gardening, cooking, crafts, cooperative games, science fiction, and so forth—could increase the social involvement of children who have different kinds of temperaments, skills, and abilities.

INTERPERSONAL FREEDOM

Perhaps the most important implication of sociometry is that it suggests the goal of interpersonal freedom. To understand this concept, it is necessary to consider the many ways our culture assumes that people can get along with each other, no matter how they are mixed. This is a rather mechanistic idea and denies the reality of tele and the fact that people work best with others with whom they are congenial. In our contemporary age, a time characterized by realistic options for choice among subgroups, the traditional requirement that people stay with their groups of origin is obsolete. It is clearly healthier for people to be in a more open social structure that promotes free choice based on common interests, temperament, or other telic criteria.

To understand this concept, first consider the range of your acquaintance network, your extended family, neighbors, co-workers, and/or classmates; choose one group and notice your own variations in preference. Some of the people in the group have a range of interests, a level of activity, a style of playfulness, or other values or behaviors different enough so that you are not really comfortable being with them. Others seem to be naturally and effortlessly more compatible. Many are sort of in-between. What could help you to find and spend more time with the ones with whom you have the greatest rapport? Sociometry, formally or informally implemented, aims at exactly this goal.

Thus, the idea of interpersonal freedom is that it reminds us of the possibility of being with others who are enough like ourselves so that there is a free give-and-take of complementary behaviors. This can occur in relationships with positive and reciprocal tele without that subtle sense that people are having to manipulate each other in order to get their needs met. A corollary is the presence in congenial relations of a sense of relative freedom from unwanted or irrelevant expectations. Of course, I am not suggesting that reasonable obligations can be sidestepped, but rather that in freely chosen groups the members are less likely to be needing things from each other that cannot be given.

In spite of the continuing increase in opportunities for choice, it is fair to suggest that many if not most people are avoiding addressing this challenge because of the fear of losing a familiar social base and the lack of awareness that there are other groups that would be more naturally congenial. Many seem to have classically repressed the awareness that there are choices possible. Thus, in relation to group dynamics or even to the process of psychotherapy, it might be helpful to have participants consider the following issues:

- Recognizing and correctly interpreting the subtle symptoms of being "stuck" in an interpersonal context in which there is too much neutral, indifferent, or negative tele.

- Knowing the range of possibilities regarding finding others with whom one shares positive tele, and the variables involved.
- Learning how to find out about alternatives and to check out those situations.
- Knowing how to make a transition from one affiliation to another.

All of these issues involve a skill that could loosely be termed "thinking sociometrically." It involves a heightened sensitivity to noticing your own preferences and the criteria that contribute to them. Becoming aware of this dimension in yourself and others can increase your interpersonal competence, and when groups can integrate this orientation, they can develop norms that facilitate group members' finding their own natural interpersonal connections.

REFERENCES

Evans, K. M. (1962). *Sociometry and education.* London: Routledge and Kegan Paul.

Gronlund, Norman E. (1959). *Sociometry in the classroom.* New York: Harper & Bros.

Hale, Ann E. (1974). Warm-up to a sociometric exploration. *Group Psychotherapy and Psychodrama, 27,* 157–172.

Hale, Ann E. (1985). *Conducting clinical sociometric explorations: A manual for psychodramatists and sociometrists.* Roanoke, VA: Author (Royal Publishing Company, 137 W. Campbell Avenue, Roanoke, VA 24011. This is the best introduction to the method.)

Jennings, Helen Hall. (1950). *Leadership and isolation* (2nd ed.). New York: Longmans, Green.

Jennings, Helen Hall. (1959). *Sociometry in group relations: A manual for teachers* (2nd ed.). Washington, DC: American Council on Education.

Kosemihal, N. S. (1959). Sociometry and cybernetics. *Group Psychotherapy, 12,* 102–109.

Kumar V. K., & Treadwell, Thomas. (1985). *Practical sociometry for psychodramatists.* West Chester, PA: Authors.

Lindsey, Gardner, & Borgatta, Edgar F. (1954). Sociometric measurement. In Gardner Lindsey (Ed.), *Handbook of social psychology* (chapter 11). Cambridge, MA: Addison-Wesley.

Lippitt, R., Bradford, L., & Benne, K. (1947). Sociodramatic clarification of leader and group roles as a starting point for effective group functioning. *Sociatry, 1*(1), 82–91. (Author's note: Several other articles by these early pioneers of the T-group may be found around this time in early issues of Moreno's journals.)

Mendelson, Peter D. (1977). Sociometry as a life philosophy. *Group Psychotherapy, Psychodrama, and Sociometry, 30,* 70–85.

Moreno, J. L. (1934). *Who shall survive? A new approach to the problem of human interrelations.* Washington, DC: Nervous and Mental Disease Publishing Co. (Author's note: See Moreno, 1953b, revised and expanded version.)

Moreno, J. L. (1953a). Kurt Lewin and the question of paternity. *Group Psychotherapy, 5*(1–2), 1–4.

Moreno, J. L. (1953b). *Who shall survive? Foundations of sociometry, group psychotherapy and sociodrama* (2nd ed.). Beacon, NY: Beacon House.

Northway, Mary L. (1967) *A primer of sociometry* (2nd ed.). Toronto: University of Toronto Press.

PART V
Practical Foundations

14

Principles of Psychodramatic Techniques

Psychodrama in its broadest application is aimed at the liberation of creativity in individuals, groups, and organizations (Ortman, 1966). To this end, almost any of the methods may be considered as long as they are constructive and the welfare of the group or individual is maintained. The principles presented in this book help to guide the practitioner in choosing appropriate techniques, and some of the essential themes that underlie the many variations include the following (and these can be combined):

- Use physical action, rather than narrative (i.e., showing a situation rather than talking about it).
- Use direct address, talking to the people most involved (or auxiliaries playing their roles), rather than about them.
- Recognize that the active behavior of others in enacted scenes evokes more spontaneous and direct behavior.

- Make abstract situations more concrete, working with specific scenes.
- Promote authentic encounters whenever possible.
- Encourage participants to make affirmative statements about desires, fears, intentions, using sentences beginning with "I."
- Deal with situations in the past or future as if they were happening in the present moment, the here-and-now.
- Value the potential for redecisions, renegotiations, and corrective experiences in the present.
- Include attention to nonlexical components (e.g., voice tone, inflection, intensity, pacing) and nonverbal components (e.g., position, gesture, expression, rhythm) in communications.
- Have participants directly exercise empathic skills through role reversal (an operationalized technique for using the Golden Rule).
- Work toward increasing levels of self-disclosure and honesty, especially about feelings.
- Respect and implement interpersonal preferences in the course of working with group dynamics.
- Methodically assess and give feedback to groups regarding their collective preferences to help them to deal with their own tasks of cohesion and conflict resolution (i.e., sociometry).
- Include a degree of playfulness in a situation.
- Vary the identity of the participants (e.g., the person playing a symbolic role) or situation to reduce overinvolvement and to stimulate the sense of alternative possibilities.
- Utilize symbols and metaphors, personifying them and making them more vivid.
- Include other artistic principles and vehicles, such as movement, staging, costuming, poetry, art, music or sound, lighting.
- Exaggerate or amplify behavior to explore a wider range of responses.
- Recognize and utilize the nature and value of the warming-up process as a precursor to creative behavior.
- Use the vehicle of dramatic techniques and the reality-expanding context of drama for exploring and expressing the experiences of the imagination as well as actual situations (i.e., make the phenomenal concrete).
- Address and enhance the processes of excitement, enthusiasm, and vitality.

- Actively utilize and cultivate sublimation as a channel for creative energies, thus offering alternatives for "neurotic" and characterological dynamics.
- Utilize the therapeutic factors of group therapy.

These principles have as their key purpose the promotion of spontaneity, which refers not to mere impulsiveness but rather to a refined receptivity to and effective application of creative intuitions and insights. In this sense, psychodrama can be used along with other psychotherapeutic approaches, behavioristic, guided fantasy, hypnosis, Gestalt therapy, bioenergetic analysis, and the other creative arts or recreational therapies (Corsini, 1967; Shapiro, 1978).

The techniques of psychodrama may be classified into four general categories: Basic, Different Scenes, Conflict Resolution, and Warm-ups. A short sampling of specific approaches is noted under each.

Basic techniques used for facilitating most processes:

enactment	doubling	amplification
autodrama	soliloquy	concretization
replay	multiple ego	role reversal
asides	mirror	use of the auxiliary

Different scenes used for warm-ups and action work:

crib scene	death scene	future projection
magic shop	dream work	behind the back

Conflict resolution techniques:

role playing	role training	structured negotiation
breaking in	spectrogram	coming together nonverbally

Warm-up techniques:

auxiliary chair	shared secrets	action sociometry

General spontaneity training methods:

art, collage	theater games	sensory awakening

| guided fantasy | poetry | structured experiences |
| movement | dance | music, rhythm |

These techniques, developed by Moreno and various other psychodramatists over the last 50 years, can be applied not only in classical psychodramas but also, in modified form, in less formal contexts. I see their major potential as agents for facilitating the processes of psychotherapy with individuals, couples, families, and groups and in the ongoing therapeutic milieus of psychiatric hospitals, day treatment centers, and residential treatment centers. Family members, nurses, and other patients can function as auxiliaries in individual therapy as well as in groups, or the creative use of the empty chair can fulfill some of these role positions. It will be obvious that many of the following techniques require a group for support, but consider the possibility of modifying or adapting these ideas in working with individuals or couples. The essential principle is that of utilizing the power of imagination in a more focused fashion.

Psychodramatic techniques can be applied in a variety of ways. The following techniques are useful in clarifying the patient's attitudes and feelings: the double, the multiple ego, multiple doubling, asides, and the soliloquy. In addition, interactions can also be clarified by using the techniques of reenactment, role reversal, the mirror, and behind the back. Aspects of a problem can be dramatized by using the techniques of action sociometry.

Past events may be explored as if they were in the present, and patients can experience such themes as co-creating the scene that would most ideally fulfill their desires. Of course, this challenges them to explicitly express and own these desires, a process that is often central to the progress of psychotherapy. This technique is called act completion. If the patient wants to change the enactment, use the technique of replay, using alternative variables of an issue or scene. There are times when it is important for patients to really understand the probable motivations and attitudes of someone from their past, and the technique of role reversal can be invaluable in working through these complexes.

Speaking of the challenge of clarifying goals, this essential component of personal growth is frequently clouded by ambiguities and unconsciously motivated vagueness. Simple discussion of issues too easily gets trapped by such forms of self-deception. The future-projection technique generates a concrete example, and the issues involved can be identified and tested as to their realistic values. The magic shop is another technique that can catalyze discussion about goals and the price that must be paid for their achievement.

The role of metaphor as a valuable element in therapy is being recognized more widely, in hypnosis, family therapy, and other contemporary approaches. Psychodramatic techniques may be utilized for exercising the patient's capacity for working within metaphorical images: Concretization allows patients to experience physically what had been experienced psychologically, and the marshaling of the multilevel resources of the body can serve as a vehicle for spontaneity and insight. Re-enacting fantasies, hallucinations, and dreams utilizes the psychodramatic category of surplus reality to bring forth the unspoken feelings and attitudes that accompany the patient's fantasies.

Various warm-up techniques are appropriate to use for developing a sense of safety, a working alliance, and some increasing involvement with the issues at hand. For example, use of structured experiences as simple as having the patients pair up in order to get to know each other and then introducing each other in a group creates group cohesion. In family therapy this can be used by having one member simply tell the therapist about the other person in a noncomplaining fashion. Other introductory techniques can bring up material in an indirect fashion: Art therapy experiences, brief role playing of related (but not too emotionally loaded) situations, theater games, use of guided imagery, sensory awakening exercises, and approaches that challenge the patients' spontaneity can break the ice and give the participants a shared experience that then serves as the focus for discussion. I find that structured warm-ups can lead to even more fruitful material and move rapidly to the patient's concerns. This approach contrasts with the stereotyped gambit of relative or absolute passivity on the part of the therapist. Nevertheless, the therapist can think in terms of principles of depth psychology and utilize the best concepts from psychoanalytic and neoanalytic theory.

In working through various issues, a variety of techniques can help to sharpen discriminations. For example, using the technique of exaggeration allows for an exploration of the range of responses, from the restrained to the outrageously overexpressive. A part of a scene can be intensified by having the patient and/or the supporting players portray their roles in the most emotional, idealized, crude, ridiculous, silly, or tragic fashions. The style is chosen to open and widen the patient's sense of the range of alternatives, however implausible they may seem at first.

All of these techniques are ways of utilizing the resources of imagination, playfulness, and creativity in the human mind. It is more than a matter of simple understanding or insight; some constructive activity is also needed. A comparison of Freud's and Moreno's approaches might be illustrated by the following analogy: If Freud could be thought of as an explorer of the new territory of the mind (he at one point even likened himself to a Columbus), then Moreno might be thought of as one who developed technologies for building roads, cultivating the land, and the like. His challenge was to utilize the untapped resources of the mind and the social system. These approaches can be applied in the "superficial" arenas of ordinary consciousness, in education, recreation, and community work; or they can be applied in the depth psychological dimensions, in dynamic psychotherapy. I see psychodrama as a facilitating agent to other therapies, analogous to the impact of power tools in carpentry. The therapist's judgment is still the key factor, and the methodology cannot be effective in untrained hands.

In summary, the range of psychodramatic techniques is potentially endless. As you read about and try out the various approaches, feel free to modify the techniques of others—refine them, experiment with them, create new ones. Depending on the context and population, adapt techniques from the fields of improvisational theater (Spolin, 1963); creative drama (McCaslin, 1984; Polsky, 1980); drama therapy (Jennings, 1986); organizational development or structured experiences in therapy (Morris & Cinnamon, 1974, 1975; Pfeiffer & Jones, 1969–1974, 1972–1975; Saretsky, 1977; Timmins, 1971); play therapy; and the other creative arts therapies (Costonis, 1978; Espenak, 1981). Integrate these approaches with other methods of therapy and explore applications with a variety of populations and in a variety of contexts. When you discover or create some techniques you find helpful, please write them up and share them with others in the professional journals! Broadening the resources of the therapist, group facilitator, or educator is one of the best ways we can contribute to finding more effective approaches to increasing personal and social harmony.

REFERENCES

Corsini, Raymond J. (1967). *Role playing in psychotherapy.* Chicago: Aldine Press.

Costonis, Maureen Needham. (Ed.). (1978). *Therapy in motion.* Urbana, IL: University of Illinois Press.

Espenak, Liljan. (1981). *Dance therapy: Theory and applications.* Springfield, IL: Charles C. Thomas.

Jennings, Sue. (1986). *Creative drama in group work.* London: Winslow Press.

McCaslin, Nellie. (1984). *Creative dramatics in the classroom.* New York: David McKay Co.

Morris, Kenneth T., & Cinnamon, Kenneth M. (1974). *A handbook of verbal group exercises.* Springfield, IL: Charles C. Thomas.

Morris, Kenneth T., & Cinnamon, Kenneth M. (1975). *A handbook of non-verbal group exercises.* Springfield, IL: Charles C. Thomas.

Ortman, Harriet. (1966). How psychodrama fosters creativity. *Group Psychotherapy, 19*(3–4), 201–213.

Pfeiffer, J. W., & Jones, J. E. (1969–1974). *A handbook of structured experiences for human relations training* (Vols. 1–5 and Reference Guide). La Jolla, CA: University Associates.

Pfeiffer, J. W., & Jones, J. E. (1972–1975). *Annual handbooks for group facilitators.* La Jolla, CA: University Associates.

Polsky, Milton. (1980). *Let's improvise.* Englewood Cliffs, NJ: Prentice-Hall.

Saretsky, Ted. (1977). *Active techniques in group psychotherapy.* New York: Jason Aronson.

Shapiro, J. L. (1978). *Methods of group psychotherapy and encounter: A tradition of innovation.* Itasca, IL: F. E. Peacock.

Spolin, Viola. (1963). *Improvisations for the theater.* Evanston, IL: Northwestern University Press.

Timmins, Lois. (1972). *Understanding through communication: Structured experiments in self-exploration.* Springfield, IL: Charles C. Thomas. (Author's note: Mainly verbal techniques.)

15

A Compendium
of Psychodramatic Terms
and Techniques

Books by Kipper (1986), Goldman and Morrison (1984), and Blatner (1973) and articles by Z. Moreno (1959), Weiner and Sacks (1969), and others list many psychodramatic techniques. Kipper's book is exceptional in its presentation of a useful explanation regarding the indications for the various techniques. Let the following list stimulate your own modifications, and then write them up and publish them! (Note: We have chosen to use masculine pronouns when referring to a single protagonist.)

Act completion This validates protagonists' emotional experiences and sense of active choice by enabling them to experience psychodramatically the fulfillment of a wish, the positive resolution of a dream or conflict, or the recreation of a successful culmination of a previously frustrated or inhibited plan. Another term for this is act gratification. For example, a traumatic or disappointing scene from childhood might be replayed with the elements changed: A co-therapist or another group member takes the role of a "perfect" parent or teacher. This technique offers a more direct mode for what Franz Alexander called the "corrective emotional experience" without having the therapist get involved directly in gratifying the patient's needs.

Act hunger This refers to the inner need, conscious or unconscious, to experience some dimension of emotion or physical action by actually enacting a situation where such self-expression would be part of appropriate role behavior. For example, the need to be triumphant might evoke a scene of being a knight in combat.

Action sociogram (action sociometry) Protagonists portray their perception of the relationships in their families, work settings, the present group, or some other situation as if it were a diorama or sculpture. Distances (far or close) are shown concretely, and feelings are represented in the way people face and by physical gestures. Virginia Satir uses this technique under the name family sculpture. It also has been called statue building (Seabourne, 1963).

Advice giving The protagonist either receives or gives advice to a significant other, such as a deceased parent or a child who is leaving home.

Amplification The protagonist's softly spoken words are repeated loudly by a double or by the director; this is especially helpful in a moderately large group setting (Ossorio & Fine, 1957). Alternatively, the protagonist is encouraged to repeat with greater intensity any words softly spoken, and/or to say more about a given idea or feeling. Sometimes the double helps in this process.

Asides In the course of an interaction the protagonist makes comments directed at the audience and, using direction of head or holding up a hand, indicates that the other person in the interaction ordinarily would not be privy to these disclosures. Thus, hidden thoughts and feelings may be expressed in parallel to overtly expressed thoughts. (This has also been called therapeutic soliloquy.)

Audience This is usually a therapy group but could be any kind of group, a family, several therapists or staff members, some friends, and so on. It includes those present who are not playing a specific role in a given enactment itself, though, as noted below, the audience sometimes plays a collective role. In most cases the audience consists of fewer than 20 patients. Psychodramas can be effective with as few as 4 or 5 patients, though I suspect that around 8 to 12 is closer to the optimum. Moreno used to do open sessions with more than 100 audience members, but this was a controversial practice because of the lack of follow-up and of the lack of adequate group cohesion that could protect confidentiality. Psychodramatic methods can be effectively applied in a modified form with only one other person present and even in the dyadic therapeutic relationship.

Audience analyst   One of the group members takes the role of attending to the dynamics going on in the audience (i.e., the rest of the group) while an enactment is progressing. His function is to act as an observer and to report his feelings to the group regarding the audience's reaction to the psychodrama (Weiner & Sacks, 1969).

Autodrama   The protagonist directs the enactment and also plays the major parts. Auxiliaries may be used as helpers. (This technique is slightly different from monodrama.)

Auxiliary chair   See *Empty chair.*

Auxiliary (ego)   Directors in some cases can help protagonists experience situations more vividly than if they were to engage in a simple monodrama by using co-therapists or other people in the group. (In the last few years, Zerka Moreno has preferred to use the simpler term "auxiliary," without the added "ego," and I agree with her idea. However, in most of the earlier books, the equivalent term was auxiliary ego.)

Auxiliary person   A group member takes a potential role, walking back and forth on stage. The director says, "Here is a person in your life; it could be either sex or any age. Go up and interact in whatever way occurs to you." This is a warm-up, similar to the use of the empty chair; however, the auxiliary is used immediately, allowing for more dynamic interaction. For example, in one enactment, the person became a brother who died in Vietnam, which was then followed by a psychodramatic grief work process (Eya Fechin Branham, 1975, personal communication).

Auxiliary world   The group and even the actual milieu is structured to recreate the protagonist's phenomenological experience. For example, Zerka Moreno wrote about a patient who had a delusion that he was Jesus Christ, so he was assigned a number of auxiliaries, played by co-therapists or staff members, who enacted the roles of disciples and similar figures. He played out various rituals until he was able to begin to let go of the need to always stay in role.

Axiodrama   Issues of ethics, cosmic relationships, or values are explored. For instance, protagonists can review their relationship with God, a tempter, Satan, a guiding spirit, death, the future (personified), or perfection. (See *Judgment scene.*)

Behind the back The protagonist goes to a corner of the room and turns away from the group. The group proceeds to discuss him as if he was not there. Another variation involves the protagonist's presenting a scene or situation; then the group discusses the issues rather than the person. In a third variation the group is instructed to turn away from the protagonist and to make no response, no matter how provoked, while the protagonist is allowed to talk about his feelings toward each of them (Corsini, 1953).

Breaking in (also called "plunging in circle") Protagonists portray their efforts to cope with feelings of isolation or to engage their inner feelings by trying forcibly (but not violently) to enter a circle of six to eight group members who are facing inward and holding together (Weiner & Sachs, 1981).

Breaking out (also called "pressure circle") For a protagonist who feels trapped, the group encircles him, grasps each other's arms, and presses the protagonist in the middle, trying to keep him there, not letting him escape. He then tries to break out of the circle by any method he sees fit (short of violence). The protagonist may name his particular pressures as he experiences them in life, or these may be described simply as a general sense of pressure. If the individual finds this kind of interaction difficult with people, chairs may be used to symbolize the same pressure circle, and he gets rid of them. The group should be no larger than six to eight people (Weiner & Sachs, 1981).

Chessboard This is a variation of the action sociogram that illustrates the range of possibilities of symbols that may be utilized to warm up protagonists to the varieties of roles in their social networks. For example, using the metaphor of a chess set, a protagonist can be the king (or whatever figure he feels is most appropriate), and he is invited to choose from the group the people whom he would want to have as his bishops, queen, knights, castles, and pawns. For example, it can be used to help a patient demonstrate perceptions and feelings toward other patients and staff members.

In one-to-one therapy, little chess figures may be used to portray an action sociogram on a board. Alternatively, coins of various denominations, different kinds of hand puppets, and other varied sets of objects can become sets of a range of symbolic figures that represent the perceptions of the different roles in a patient's social atom.

Chorus   The audience or a subgroup of auxiliaries is instructed to repeat certain phrases as if they were the modern psychological equivalent of the ancient Greek chorus. Repeating the haunting reproaches, doubts, or other anxiety-provoking words or lines can deepen the protagonist's experience. Supportive statements may be used when the process is moving toward a healthier integration.

Closure   Following the action, the director should see to it that the players have an opportunity to "de-role" by talking about their expressions in role and giving themselves some distance from those events. Having them get up and "shake off" the character is often useful. The sharing should be managed so that it does not turn into an analysis of the protagonist's problem. Allow a good deal of time for this process.

Coaching   In the course of an enactment, the director may function as a coach, suggesting to the protagonist or the auxiliaries variations in approach, body posture, pacing of voice, or role definition. Perhaps one of the group members may be assigned this role of coach for the protagonist. In a role-playing setting, the main actor becomes the agent (or auxiliary) for the group, playing a scene not as he might feel it should be done but according to the directions of the group. One person at a time or the entire group may then coach the players as they enact the situation.

Concretization   Psychodrama works in part by helping patients to convert their abstract statements into something more concrete because vagueness is a major way of avoiding dealing with issues directly. The first way to do this is to have general issues such as "conflict with authorities" be transformed into a specific scene, a situation with a boss or parent or teacher in the patient's life. Another way of concretizing issues is to convert metaphors into actualities: Thus, "I wish they'd get off my back" can be enacted by having an auxiliary gently hang onto the protagonist's back. Feelings of isolation can be enhanced by having the audience withdraw some distance, turning down the lights, or perhaps using the technique of breaking in.

Crib Scene   The entire group (ideally, fewer than 12 people) is allowed to have an experience as if the group members are infants being soothingly comforted and rocked to sleep after a satisfying meal. They lie down on a soft, carpeted floor or on mats, in a comfortable position, perhaps with blankets over them. The therapist/director and perhaps one or two co-therapists go around and gently pat and stroke the "sleeping" group members as they hypnotically say things like "The mother loves the baby, takes care of the baby, such a wonderful baby. . . ." This goes on for at least 10 minutes, and then the group is aroused very gently in role: "So the baby begins to wake up, begins to move a little, stretches a little. . . ." Finally, the participants are de-roled and brought back to themselves. It is a form of hypnosis, and similar rules apply. Suggestions should be made clearly, supportively, and at a leisurely pace (Allen, 1969).

Cutting the action The process of an enactment may be stopped if the participants fall hopelessly out of role or block and are unable to continue, whenever the episode comes to a conclusion, or whenever the director sees the opportunity to stimulate thinking to a higher level of creativity by using a different episode or technique. (The phrase is derived from the old movie cliché of the director calling *"Cut!"*) The new direction is made, and the enactment continues. A similar command, "Freeze," may indicate that a very minor adjustment is needed. The actors are expected to hold the momentum of their physical and emotional positions and then resume their behavior (except for the minor adjustment) as if nothing had interrupted them. One application of this technique is in situations where the director thinks a protagonist is becoming too angry and in danger of losing control. Another indication is a scene becoming confusing and muddled. It suggests the possibility of leaving an interaction, standing "outside," in a sense, and reflecting on alternative strategies.

Dance and **Movement** The protagonist may be encouraged or permitted to move nonverbally in a scene in order to express emotion more fully or to warm up to a scene. Incidentally, in the 1940s and 1950s, Marian Chace's pioneering work in dance therapy was done in coordination with the psychodrama program at St. Elizabeth's Hospital in Washington, DC (see *Music, Singing, and Rhythm*).

Death scene The protagonist speaks to a significant other (played by an auxiliary) who is dying or has died and is in a casket; or, alternatively, the protagonist plays the dead person and is spoken to by the group members. This is a powerful technique and generally requires that the protagonist be fully warmed up (Siroka & Schloss, 1968).

Directed dialogue Emunah (1983) suggests an evocative technique in which group members experiment with a variety of ways of using specific phrases. After pairing up as dyads, each person is given one or two phrases that may be said repeatedly but with a free variation of voice tone, expression, or gesture. Evocative phrases might include "I have to go" versus "I want you to stay"; "I want it" versus "You can't have it"; or "There's something I have to tell you" versus "I don't want to hear it."

Director   In psychodrama or role playing the director is the person who facilitates the process of enactment. Usually, the director is the group leader or the patient's therapist, but sometimes a visiting consultant directs while the therapist becomes part of the audience. There may also be a co-director or an assistant director to help with the various component roles.

Double   The protagonist is joined by an auxiliary, either a trained co-therapist or a group member, whose role is to function as a support in presenting the protagonist's position or feelings. Doubles should first work toward establishing an empathic bond with the protagonist. In general, they stand to the side of and at a slight angle to the protagonist so that they can replicate the non-verbal communications and present a kind of "united front." The double is one of the most important and basic techniques in psychodrama (Leveton, 1977).

Double protagonist session   (see *Multiple protagonists*) Relationships can be explored with both parties present and involved, such as a married couple, a patient and a nurse, a parent and a child, and so on.

Dream presentation   These may be enacted as if they were happening in the present moment. Auxiliaries portray other figures, both animate and inanimate. Unfinished dreams may be completed in order to clarify fears and to introduce an affirmation of a positive chosen resolution (Moreno, 1958). Psychodrama is a good vehicle for this process of extending both dreams and guided fantasies to enhance the inner experience. James Hillman has invited us all to "dream the dream onward" (1979), and Moreno declared, "I teach them to dream again."

Ego building   An honest discussion of the protagonist is carried on by the group while the protagonist quietly faces the group and listens. The group focuses on only the positive qualities. The director stops the discussion once the group has run dry and ascertains how the recipient feels (as well as how the group feels, having said what they did). Any members of the group who desire this experience should be given the same opportunity (Feinberg, 1959).

Empty chair   (also known as "auxiliary chair")   Instead of another person (an auxiliary) playing the complementary figure in a protagonist's enactment, an empty chair represents that position.

Sometimes this allows for a more spontaneous expression of aggressive or tender feelings, depending on the makeup of the group or the embarrassment of the patient in working with another person (Lippitt, 1958). This is an invaluable technique in a one-to-one therapeutic context and has been incorporated as an integral part of Gestalt therapy.

Enactment Group members are encouraged to portray their life situations in dramatic form, to physically enact the encounters that have existed only in their memories or fantasies. Thus, the person whose situation is the focus of the group becomes the protagonist and is helped to experience the process of working with the attitudes and feelings in an action format. Enactments can be in the past (memories, redoing experiences), the present, or the future (worries, hopes, testing possible scenarios, fantasies.)

Family psychodrama The therapist or director works with immediate family members or even an extended family group, using role reversal, future projection, and any other appropriate psychodramatic techniques. The family members learn to serve as auxiliaries for each other. This approach includes teaching the family the skills of role reversal as a way of building interpersonal empathic concern, and it has major benefits for the participants. Psychodramatic methods can be powerful diagnostic, therapeutic, and educational tools, significantly increasing the effectiveness of family therapy (Remer, 1986). Psychodrama is also very useful in multiple family group therapy.

Final empty chair During the sharing portion of a psychodrama, audience members may have reactions to people in their own lives who are similar to the main roles in the preceding enactment. In order to complete their "spectator catharsis," they engage in a mini-enactment, encountering the figures in the original protagonist's drama and/or the figures in their own lives. The presentation may be angry, sad, or reconciling; it may or may not include role reversals with the person represented by the empty chair (Speros, 1972).

Fishbowl The group divides in two: Half sit in a circle facing the inside of the "fishbowl" and engage in some task or discussion; the other half sit outside and observe the dynamics. (The two halves may then change positions as a second part of the exercise.) Outside people may also be asked to function as doubles for the ones on the inside (Fine, 1968).

Freeze See *Cutting the action.*

Future projection A specific scene in the future is elaborated and may include subscenes such as the most hoped-for outcome, the most feared event, an exaggerated reaction, a realistic expectation, or just an exploration of some of the dimensions of a forthcoming situation. In role training, this technique becomes an opportunity for rehearsal and behavioral practice (Yablonsky, 1954).

Gibberish   To facilitate self-observation and the group's observation of the nonverbal elements in an interpersonal interaction, have the major parties involved (or just the protagonist and the auxiliary) replay a scene or continue an enactment using nonsense syllables instead of real words. They could use complex syllables that sound like a foreign language or simply say "blah blah blah" or "yakkety yak yak" or "da da da da da." The point is that they repeat the expression of emotion in the interaction with the same facial expressions, intonations, and gestures but are free of the distraction of the content of the words.

Goodbye scenes   These are used to complete unfinished business and as an important part of grief work (Blatner, 1985a pp.61–72). (See also *Death scene.*)

Guided fantasy   This is a method catalyzed by verbal suggestions from the director. The protagonist is relaxed and experiences in imagination a series of events partly suggested by the director. Psychodramatic techniques may be modified and applied to help the protagonist cope with situations as they arise. This approach has been used by Roberto Assagioli in his method of psychosynthesis and also by Leuner, Desoille, Schutz, Schoor, and many others. It may also be applied to the group as a whole, lying randomly scattered around the room or in a circle with their heads together. It can be a useful warm-up or closing technique. Some of the themes used include a trip through the body or into the sea and investigating a strange building or castle (Samuels & Samuels, 1975, pp. 181–207).

Hallucinatory psychodrama   Patients portray the phenomena of their hallucinations or delusions, just as is done with dream work. The different sources of voices become personalized and elaborated, and alternative outcomes are explored (Moreno, 1958). The use of this technique requires good clinical judgment.

High chair   The protagonist or the auxiliary is placed on a platform or in a tall chair. If the protagonist is elevated, he may have the courage to make assertions himself in a more confident manner. If the auxiliary is elevated, the protagonist may experience addressing an authority figure. This technique is similar to the use of a balcony if it is available.

Hypnodrama   A psychodrama is enacted after first inducing a mild state of trance in the protagonist and perhaps even the group. A therapist who uses this method should have adequate training in hypnotherapy (Greenberg, 1977, pp. 231–303).

Idealizations   A protagonist may portray his ideal self in a scene, and this role may also be used for dialogue with other parts of his identity. The ideal other, as parent, child, or mate, may be created by using surplus reality, usually in order to engage in a scene of act completion. For example, a protagonist may become his ideal parent in an act of reparenting or may experience an ideal mother or father in a scene where he is reparented. The prop of a rocking chair is often useful for such scenes.

Identity   A protagonist chooses two auxiliaries, one to represent himself and the other to represent his "negative identity" —that is, a person he hates, despises, or just dislikes. (Alternatively, he can compare his own present sense of himself with his ideal self.) Then, as the protagonist lists essential differences, the two auxiliaries, starting back to back in the center of the room, take a step apart. If the protagonist mentions a similarity rather than a difference, the auxiliaries retrace a step.

An alternative technique may be used to clarify and reduce transference phenomena. If the protagonist is treating his wife like his mother, his therapist like his minister, himself like his father, or any other two figures in his life, have him do a similar technique, starting with the two auxiliaries standing several feet apart. With each stated similarity they take one step together, and with each stated difference they take one step apart (Miller, 1972).

In situ   Moreno wrote of applying psychodrama in the very situation in which the conflict might be occurring—on the spot, so to speak. This might be in the home, in the schoolyard, at work, or on the street. The idea of doing family therapy in the family's home is an example of this idea, but if Moreno had done it, he would probably have had the family use their kitchen and bedrooms to enact scenes, as well as the living room.

Instant sociometry   In a large group, after some general action warm-ups, have the people mill around looking for a "family." The directions are to constitute yourself into a family grouping. What that ends up consisting of becomes a source for further discussion and enactment.

Intensification   Goldman and Morrison (1984) note that feelings can be made more intense and explicit by using a variety of techniques, such as echoing or repeating the main message of a situation or a verbalized expression of a feeling, having protagonists put their bodies in the shape of their feeling, or locating the feeling in their bodies. I sometimes intensify an action sociogram by having the various people in the protagonist's social atom surround him and converge on him slowly, each speaking his particular message. Thus, a person who feels caught in the middle or torn apart can experience this form of concretization by having the auxiliaries who are playing the roles of their social atom pull, pick, or press on them, saying the lines ever more insistently and loudly until the protagonist feels overwhelmed and has a catharsis of emotion that prepares him for further work toward integration.

Judgment scene   The protagonist presents a conflict in terms of a courtroom scene, perhaps in the mind, perhaps in heaven as a final judgment. This is useful if the protagonist feels guilty, is judging himself, or is complaining of being judged by others. In this context, behaviors and beliefs may be subjected to a dialectical process, which is dramatized by having the protagonist and auxiliaries take the various roles of prosecutor, defense attorney, defendant, judge, jury, and so on. Some of the disputation process suggested by Albert Ellis in his method of rational-emotive therapy may be done within this enactment context (Sacks, 1967).

Letter   The protagonist writes an imaginary letter to or reads one from a significant other. This is useful as a warm-up, allowing a little distance before moving on to an actual psychodramatic encounter. As a closure, it can carry the feeling of resolution: The protagonist puts into the context of letter writing some advice or acknowledgment to the other person in a relationship, or he reads the kind of letter he secretly wishes he might receive (Sacks, 1974).

Lighting   Colored lights and dimmers can enhance the effectiveness of many enactments. Certain scenes are made more vivid when enacted primarily under red light (e.g., hell, anger); amber light (e.g., a tawdry or sleazy event); blue light (e.g., introspective, heaven, dreamlike, depressed); relative darkness (e.g., shameful, intimate, isolated); green light (e.g., envious, deceitful), and so on. Protagonists may participate in requesting the kind of lighting they wish. Time of day and locale may be factors also in determining the lighting. (However useful they may be if available, theatrical props are not necessary for doing psychodrama. Nor is a formal stage required. The suggestion of a place in a room where people can enact a situation suffices, and in this sense, "the stage is enough." The mobilization of action in therapy can occur in the simplest of contexts, and this always takes precedence over any technical additions.)

Magic shop One at a time, group members bargain with a "shopkeeper" who can grant their fondest desire. Often, a little playful elaboration of the mysterious setting and the potential magical qualities of the shopkeeper sets the mood. Group members in the audience can be enlisted to help ensure that the bargains or exchanges have some degree of poetic justice (Blatner, 1973, pp. 40–42).

Masks These may be used to provide even more role distance and facilitate the sense that it is the role rather than the person that is active in a situation—thus, it facilitates sociodrama. On a personal level, Landy (1985) describes a technique in which the protagonist prepares by ritually constructing four masks of gauze-impregnated plaster of paris based on the configuration of his own face, then molds or decorates them so that they come to represent self, both parents, and one sibling. These become vehicles for a modified action sociogram encounter: Each figure is "interviewed," the protagonist playing their parts, and then the protagonist engages them in an enacted encounter. The idea of using masks should be considered more often as a synthesis of art and psychodrama.

Mirror The protagonist stands back and watches while the role he portrayed is replayed by an auxiliary. A family interaction may also be mirrored, or a parent can watch a scene from his own childhood as a way of gaining insight regarding his own parenting behavior. This is a human version of videotape playback. It can be a powerful confrontational technique and must be used with discretion. The protagonist must not be made the object of ridicule. The technique of role reversing, to give protagonists feedback regarding the impact of their nonverbal behavior, is a little like the mirror technique (Torrance, 1978).

Monodrama The patient plays all of the parts of the enactment. The advantage here is the access gained to the protagonist's viewpoint. It also requires no auxiliaries and may be part of individual therapy. A third advantage is that it guides the protagonist into broadening his perspective through role reversal. It is often used with the empty chair technique, and the protagonist physically moves into another seat when taking a different role. A disadvantage is the absence of the stimulation that can come from an auxiliary's behavior. Fritz Perls's technique of Gestalt therapy was essentially an adaptation of the monodramatic technique.

Moving feelings   If protagonists are blocked in their emotions, the director helps them notice where they are feeling tension. If it is in a part of the body that cannot be put into action, a suggestion is made that the feelings move to another part of the body that can be more expressive. For example, anger in the stomach may be moved to anger in the fists, or tears in the heart can move to tears in the eyes (Goldman & Morrison, 1984).

Multiple double   The protagonist is given two or more doubles who help express different parts of the self. These can represent various aspects, such as the self in the future, present, and past; "good" and "bad" selves; Eric Berne's description of the Parent, Adult, and Child; or Fritz Perls's Topdog and Underdog (Z. Moreno, 1959).

Multiple ego   The protagonist uses empty chairs or positions on the stage to represent different parts of the self, such as conscience and temptation. Then, playing the various roles that are now separated in space—with or without the help of auxiliaries— the protagonist has the parts present their positions and encounter each other. This is quite useful in concretizing internal conflicts (Blatner, 1985b, pp. 29–42).

Multiple protagonists   (See *Family psychodrama, Double protagonist*)   Psychodrama may be used to catalyze more authentic encounters and to generate creative problem solving among several people, such as members of a family or a small group. In this sense, Moreno was doing "conjoint therapy" (a prelude to family therapy) in the 1930s. Active systems-oriented family therapy skills are closely related to those used in leading psychodrama groups.

Music, Singing, and **Rhythm**   There are numerous activities and techniques that can be used as warm-ups or for closure (see *Dance*).

Nonverbal techniques   During a psychodrama, dance, music, pantomime, touch, and other ways of using the dimension of nonverbal communications can offer powerful vehicles for helping to bypass habitual verbal patterns of defense and constriction (see *Dance, Music,* and *Touch*).

Nonverbally coming together   Two persons who need to become acquainted in a new way or to work out some mild conflict go to opposite sides of the room. They remove their glasses and shoes and then walk toward each other. When they come together, they may interact in any way they wish, responding spontaneously in the moment, but no words are to be spoken. Nonviolence is maintained, and they stop when they sense they are finished. Afterward, the two parties and the group may discuss their perceptions of and feelings about doing or seeing the event (Schutz, 1971).

Nonviolence   A fundamental precept of psychodrama is the contractual agreement of the group to do no bodily harm to one another. Psychodrama is an active modality at times and involves verbal and physical expressions of feeling, including fantasies of violence. The directors and group members take responsibility for channeling these feelings into activities that symbolically express the feelings, such as having mattresses, pillows, or foam-rubber bats (*batacas*) to pound with or on. The director has the participants pause and remove glasses, shoes, and jewelry, which communicates a clear, comfortable sense that no harm is to occur to anyone. Techniques such as slow motion have been devised, which reflect the willingness to sustain a protagonist's intensity while still protecting everyone from harm.

Personification   Roles of inanimate objects (such as a person's writing desk or a family's living room couch), pets or other animals, abstract ideas, parts of one's body, the generalized other (i.e., "them"); all may be portrayed by an auxiliary as if they had subjectivity and feelings.

Photograph warm-up   The director has the group remember a photograph that is important, noting who is in it. This is a powerfully evocative technique that can then lead into a kind of action sociogram by portraying the picture. The implied thoughts and statements of the participants are expressed, and, in turn, an encounter or psychodrama may ensue.

Planned psychodrama   There are several levels of planning. Simply arranging for a psychodrama session, or scheduling them at regular intervals, is the most common form. Another level involves the actual planning of certain elements in a forthcoming psychodrama. For example, the therapist might agree to work with a patient on a particular issue in the next psychodrama session. An even more specific form of planning can happen; for example, the patient, therapist, and director may decide certain details ahead of time, such as the setting of an opening scene or the choice of certain trusted auxiliaries. Even though some elements are planned, there is still much room for spontaneous development in the course of the enactment.

Props   Psychodrama sessions can be facilitated by a few props, such as some lightweight chairs, a small table, some pads, blankets, pillows, foam-rubber bats ("encounter bats," or *batacas*), a rocking chair, a soft fiber rope (which can represent "the tie that binds" in an enmeshed relationship), something sturdy to stand on, and so on. Props can help maintain nonviolence, enhance enactment, and facilitate a protagonist's warm-up. However, as discussed in *Lighting*, psychodrama can be managed without them.

Protagonist This is a term used in psychodrama to indicate the person playing the principal role in an enactment. The protagonist presents the issue to be explored, and it is this person's experience that becomes the central focus of the group. The reason for using a term other than "patient" is that when a person becomes a protagonist he can play a number of roles besides himself. For the purposes of clarity, therefore, the term refers to the person who is the focus of an enactment. During a more general group session, the protagonist can change from one person to another, but each shift requires a whole new scene, goal, and, so to speak, a new "therapeutic contract."

Protagonists in a psychodramatic exploration that includes several scenes can play themselves or significant others in their lives. They can become their own doubles, co-directors, or (in the mirror technique) their own audience. Thus, it is not the role played that represents the protagonist but the person who enacts and explores the problem. In sociodrama, the protagonist may be a representative of a group or subgroup, and the conflicts explored relate to a single dimension or role.

In addition to portraying himself, the protagonist also may take the role of a significant other in his life, a part of himself, a figure in a dream he had; but whichever role he takes, the focus remains on his experience. For example, if a protagonist portrays a scene about his marriage, and the person playing the wife (the auxiliary) begins to become emotional, she would be replaced in the scene, perhaps to be dealt with later; however, the focus would remain on the protagonist. If the protagonist reversed roles in the scene, and the auxiliary—then in the patient's role—began to take the scene in a direction different from the protagonist's actual situation, the director would check this out with the protagonist ("Is this the way you would play it?"). If it is inaccurate, the director would return the focus to the protagonist, away from the fantasy (or subjective reality) of the auxiliary playing the protagonist's original role.

Nor does the protagonist remain the same during the course of a group session—only for the period of one psychodrama at a time.

In some group sessions, for example, the protagonist may for a brief time be one of the staff members or even the therapist. If the director becomes involved in a countertransferential struggle, a short enactment with him or her as the protagonist may resolve the issue. Thus, to be a protagonist is not always the same as being in the patient role. On the other hand, the patient role really should be less fixed, and as Moreno emphasized, each person becomes an agent of healing for the other.

The reason "protagonist" is a more useful term than "patient" also involves the description of the dynamics of a session. A protagonist may play his own role, that of another patient, a relative, or his own double, whereas an auxiliary in this situation might play the role of the "physical" patient–protagonist. The protagonist becomes more flexible than in real life during a psychodrama, and this is the magic of the context of play.

Protagonist roles During a psychodrama session, a protagonist may be invited to play a variety of "process" roles: Thus, he may become his own double, director, counselor, higher self, tempter, or spectator (the last is a form of the mirror technique).

Psychodrama à deux These techniques may be applied in individual therapy, in some ways similar to Gestalt therapy, with the therapist playing the roles of director, double, and other auxiliary roles. This is a useful way to integrate the many valuable contributions of psychodrama into the traditional one-to-one therapeutic setting (Vander May, 1981).

Psychodramatic shock The protagonist is presented with an emotionally loaded situation without warning. However, this should be done when the group is fully warmed up. The director introduces this technique when it is helpful to have the protagonist deal with a painful situation, such as a wartime trauma, an announcement of a demand for a divorce or news of a death, or resurrection of a psychotic experience (i.e., a hallucination or a delusion). Of course, this technique requires a high level of skill and judgment as well as sufficient time for working through and achieving an integration. This technique is a kind of "implosive therapy" and deconditioning, replaying a traumatic scene until it loses its negative power. For example, there is an actual case of a woman who became very angry at the dinner table and told her father to drop dead—and he did. The scene was reenacted repeatedly to allow her to integrate it into her life (Z. Moreno, 1966).

Puppets, masks These can be used as aids in warming up the group. A protagonist may work with hand puppets as a way of presenting some of the elements of a situation.

Reformed auxiliary ego   After exploring a protagonist's situation and evoking the catharsis associated with discovering the pain of an unfulfilled need, it is sometimes useful to offer a corrective emotional experience. The auxiliary, who may be playing a harsh or depressed parent, for example, is instructed to portray the role in a more nurturing, validating, empathic, or supportive manner. Having the patient identify what behaviors might fulfill the unmet needs adds to the overall experience of insight (Sacks, 1970).

Rehearsed psychodrama   Occasionally patients with a creative flair might want to present a scene or series of scenes based on or related to their own lives. They adapt a piece of literature or a segment of a play, or they write, direct, rehearse, and act in a play (or skit, for it might be quite brief) of their own, with the help of trained facilitators. These can then be worked with or further explored using psychodramatic methods.

Replay   Scenes may be reenacted with changes in order to experience more ventilation, a happier ending, a more effective interpersonal strategy, a desensitized response to a frightening situation, or similar outcome. The setting, the participants, the protagonist's behavior, or another person's behavior may be varied. However, it is best to change only one variable at a time.

Role playing   The focus in role playing is on finding the best approach for a problem. It is most often used in business, industry, and education. Actually, the boundaries between role playing and sociodrama, and even psychodrama, are often blurred. In general, however, role playing is not aimed at discovering the deeper feelings involved in a person's behavior. Problem-centered role playing is more like sociodrama, because it is aimed at defining the various aspects of the problem. Method-centered role playing explores alternative strategies for dealing with the problem. Rehearsing and refining these approaches becomes role training.

Role presentation   The protagonist may present any role, including that of an inanimate object, as if it could say what it felt. Thus, a desk at home could talk to its owner about how it has been neglected, or a couch could talk to a couple about its perceptions of the couple's early courting behavior. Similarly, pets, figures in dreams, children who were never conceived or born, heavenly judges, and others all can be psychologically real in psychodrama.

Role reversal   The major participants in an interaction change roles. When a protagonist in a psychodrama role reverses, it is a way of transcending the habitual limitations of egocentricity. Role reversal is indicated when it is appropriate for the protagonist to empathize with the other person's viewpoint. Also, role reversal is used during the setting up of a scene and the warming up of an auxiliary. The protagonist reverses roles and demonstrates how the other person in the scene behaves, thus giving nonverbal cues to the auxiliary so that the scene is played relatively close to the protagonist's experience. (This is also called changing parts or switching roles.)

Role taking The act of embodying a particular role, usually one that is not part of one's ordinary life, can be done with a narrow or broad definition of how the role may be portrayed. When a person brings a fair amount of spontaneity to the role-taking process, it may be called role creativity. (In social psychology, however, this term tends to refer to something more like role reversal.)

Role training The goal is primarily to rehearse or refine a role, such as how to behave in a job interview, how to ask someone for a date, how to say no to a salesperson, and so on. The basic task is usually established at the outset, and no major effort is made to explore deep feelings involved (Seabourne, 1985).

Self-presentation A protagonist presents his home, workplace, or other essential locus for a description of the situation, along with a brief portrayal of all of the relevant people in that area of his social atom. He shows how people behave and what is said and not said; and, using various basic dramatic techniques, he portrays his own phenomenological and psychodramatic world.

Self-realization A protagonist enacts a general view of his life, including elements of the past and present, but especially showing a possible, desired, or probable future chain of events. This is an abbreviated scenario of high and low points.

Shared secrets Each group member writes a secret on a piece of paper and puts it into a container, mixed with those of everyone else. Then the secrets are picked out (each being sure not to pick out his own secret). Each person then reads the secret and elaborates on it for about 1 or 2 minutes as if it were indeed his own secret. This technique is best for a group no larger than about nine people. It is useful as a warm-up, to build group cohesion, and as a method for developing empathy.

Silent auxiliary Activities are suggested by gesture rather than speech, similar to pantomime. A variant is the silent double. At times, this role may be the ideal support for a protagonist. It can also allow a group member who is not able to think of anything to say to participate nevertheless.

Situation tests   A given situation is presented, and members of the group are invited to show how they would deal with it. Alternatively, one person is sent out, the others are helped to set up the scene, and then the person reenters and takes on the role of protagonist in the situation.

Slow motion   Actions may be enhanced, cooled down, or made more available for development by having the participants move as if they were in slow motion. The analogy to being underwater or in gelatin might be used. This technique may be combined with replay, mirror, and dream work, among others. Using a related idea that produces different results, actions can be speeded up; however, this is more limited in its usefulness with other techniques.

Sociodrama   A situation is explored in terms of a single major role relationship, such as patients and doctors, teachers and administrators, conservatives and liberals, and so on. The unique specifics and combinations of roles that make up the lives of real individuals are addressed in *psychodrama*. However, general issues relating to people in a given group offer excellent material for sociodrama. This approach is helpful in learning about or creatively exploring the possibilities inherent in the challenges of various social and other forms of roles.

Sociometry   Moreno's method of measuring the interpersonal relationships in a group can be used also as a warm-up for group interactions. The basic method employs paper and pencil and has each person note his preferred choice of other group members as partners in various activities. After these are posted in the form of a chart or diagram, the results are shared with the group. It becomes obvious who are the "stars" and who are relative isolates. The various positions become the themes for psychodramatic explorations. There are also a variety of ways of demonstrating sociometric choices without paper or pencils (see *Action sociometry*).

Soliloquy   The protagonist shares with the audience the feelings and thoughts that would normally be kept hidden or suppressed. The protagonist may be engaged in a solitary activity, such as walking home, winding down after an eventful day, or getting ready for an event in the near future. It might involve advice giving, words to bolster courage, or reproachful criticism. Variations include having the protagonist soliloquize with a double as the two of them walk around, having the protagonist talk to a pet, or converting the inner dialogue into an encounter with an empty chair or auxiliary playing a wiser, future self or another part of the personality (Z. Moreno, 1959).

Spectrogram For any issue or quality that is becoming the subject of discussion, a group can indicate where they feel they stand or how they rate themselves by making an invisible line in the room and placing themselves somewhere on that line. This technique leads to a good deal of discussion, as it objectifies and clarifies the problem. It is a one-dimensional form of action sociometry (Kole, 1967).

The stage In Moreno's opinion, the stage was originally an important part of psychodrama. He designed stages that were accessible to a small audience, consisting of a three-tiered, circular area that evoked more of a sense of dramatic action. It was an example of architecture as applied to psychology (Enneis, 1952). If enough classical psychodrama is done, it would be desirable to construct such a stage. It should be noted, however, that most psychodramas are held in far less formal contexts—in group rooms, empty conference rooms (in which the tables and chairs can be moved out of the way), or large offices. Probably an area of at least 50 sq ft is required. It is best to avoid the high stages in school or theater auditoriums because they cannot be accessed easily and are too removed from the coziness of the group. As mentioned before, the method can also be adapted for use in the relatively narrow confines of the consulting room because the action involves the patient's mode of involvement rather than any formal production.

Status nascendi This is Moreno's term for that aspect of a situation in which the dynamic elements are still coming together, when the key decisions are being made and the crucial events are occurring. The point is to move toward these critical events because they are the scenes that have the greatest potential for creative revision. Thus, a useful direction in a psychodrama is "Show us a time when things were different," before certain key changes or decisions had been made. This scene often occurs in the course of a psychodrama as the third or fourth scene in a series.

Substitute role Patients who are unwilling to portray themselves may be willing to enact a role of someone else that is in actuality related to their own situation. For example, a middle-aged woman with an agitated depression consented to play her mother, who had run a boardinghouse many years before. In this role she was at ease and seemed to enjoy being on stage. During the third session, in which she continued to play her mother, the patient brought up the fact that one of the boardinghouse roomers was promiscuous. This story was also her own story. As a young woman her actual illegitimate pregnancy was followed by an abortion. Now, as she approached middle age, she worried about this incident and felt sure her present family would find out and no longer love her. When this all came out in a psychodrama, she could see, with the help of role reversal and audience feedback, that she was actually secure in the love of her family (Parrish, 1953).

Surplus reality   One can enact not only scenes that involve the real events in one's life but also the scenes that, as Zerka Moreno has said, "have never happened, will never happen, or can never happen." These scenes often represent hopes, fears, and unfinished psychological business that are experienced as being in some ways more real than the events of everyday existence. Psychodrama permits people to use imagination as the basis of enactments, and this in turn validates our capacity to participate in experiences that are "bigger than life." Moreno called psychodrama "the Theatre of Truth" because what is really true for people includes the realms of their emotions, their fantasies, and their surplus realities.

Symbolic distance   The protagonist enacts a role that is somewhat or even very different from his real-life role, and then he is gradually led back toward playing the real role. This technique, using story-book characters, is particularly valuable when working with children. For instance, an unrelated boy and girl in treatment were both anxious about forthcoming discharges. They enacted an improvised variation of Hansel and Gretel—brother and sister facing the world. From this, they were able to generate more realistic future-projection scenes (Parrish, 1953).

Symbolic realization   Symbolic situations are enacted. For example, if the protagonist feels weighed down by problems, suggest that an auxiliary or two gently hang over his back. If the protagonist feels isolated or trapped, have him do the breaking-in or breaking-out exercise, having to relate to a group of auxiliaries in a small circle.

Telephone   This prop can evoke a good deal of interaction, especially with teenagers. The fact that it is in actuality disconnected allows for all kinds of calls to be placed or received without repercussions. Simply bringing one or two telephones out and then, after a pause, playing a hidden cassette tape of a bell ringing can bring the action alive (Emunah, 1985).

Touching   Inherent in the course of many psychodrama sessions is the use of bodily contact or touching. It may be used positively, such as in a warm handshake or an arm around a shoulder, or negatively, such as pushing away in disgust. Many people's early life experiences have been affected by the way they were led, held, stroked, and so on.

Unplanned psychodrama   This refers to responding to an event in real life as it is happening, in the here-and-now, with a psychodramatic enactment. For example, it may be used to work out conflicts in the course of an outing, at home with family members, or similar situations. This is especially effective in such settings as camps, day treatment centers, or psychiatric hospitals. (See *In situ.*)

Videotaped psychodrama   The videotaped psychodramatic experience includes being involved in an enactment, viewing the videotape of the enactment, and then replaying parts of the psychodrama that need to be worked out further. (In the past, Moreno also used audiotape recordings and cinema to help patients hear or see themselves and use that experience as a warm-up to further exploration.) (See Heilveil, 1983; Lee, 1981.)

Voluntary double   Members of the audience are encouraged or permitted to signal the director and enter as doubles (if permitted) whenever they believe they are identifying deeply with the protagonist and can facilitate the creative process. The voluntary double may remain in the action until he is dismissed by the director, or he may fade out as soon as a contribution is made (Torrance, 1978).

Warm-up   A wide variety of techniques can be used to develop group cohesion, focus a group on its task, or create a special atmosphere, orientation, or theme in a group. Individuals can also be helped to enter an area of psychological or emotional exploration, whether their own or someone else's, using techniques mentioned throughout this section (Weiner & Sacks, 1969).

REFERENCES

Allen, Doris Twitchell. (1969). The crib scene: A psychodramatic exercise. *Psychotherapy: Theory, Research, and Practice, 6,* 206–208.
Blatner, Adam. (1973). *Acting-In* (pp. 40–42). New York: Springer Publishing Co.

Blatner, Adam. (1985a). The principles of grief work. *Creating Your Living* (pp. 61–72). San Marcos, TX: Author.

Blatner, Adam. (1985b). Psychodramatic approaches to personal growth. *Creating Your Living* (pp. 29–42). San Marcos, TX: Author.

Corsini, Raymond J. (1953). The "behind your back" technique in psychodrama. *Group Psychotherapy, 6*, 102–109.

Emunah, Renee. (1983). Drama therapy with adult psychiatric patients. *The Arts in Psychotherapy, 10*, 77–84.

Emunah, Renee. (1985). Drama therapy and adolescent resistance. *The Arts in Psychotherapy, 12*, 71–79.

Enneis, James M. (1952). Establishing a psychodrama program. *Group Psychotherapy, 5*(2), 111–119.

Fine, Leon. (1968, June 28). Presentation at professional training workshop, Belmont, CA.

Feinberg, Henry. (1959). The ego building technique. *Group Psychotherapy, 12*(3–4), 230–235.

Goldman, Elaine, & Morrison, Delcy Schram. (1984). *Psychodrama: Experience and process.* Phoenix, AZ: Eldemar.

Greenberg, Ira A. (Ed.). (1977). Group hypnotherapy and hypnodrama. Chicago: Nelson-Hall.

Heilveil, Ira. (1983). *Video in mental health practice: An activities handbook.* New York: Springer Publishing Co.

Hillman, James. (1979). *Dreams and the underworld.* New York: Harper & Row.

Kipper, David. (1986). *Psychotherapy through clinical role playing.* New York: Brunner/Mazel.

Kole, Delbert. (1967). The spectrogram in psychodrama. *Group Psychotherapy, 20*(1–2), 53–61.

Landy, Robert. (1985). The image of the mask: Implications for theatre and therapy. *Journal of Mental Imagery, 9*(4), 43–56.

Lee, Richard H. (1981). Video as adjunct to psychodrama and role playing. In Jerry L. Fryrear & Bob Fleshman (Eds.), *Videotherapy in mental health* (pp. 121–145). Springfield, IL: Charles C. Thomas.

Leveton, Eva. (1977). *Psychodrama for the timid clinician.* New York: Springer Publishing Co.

Lippitt, Rosemary. (1958). Auxiliary chair technique. *Group Psychotherapy, 11*(1–2), 8–23.

Miller, Donnell. (1972). Psychodramatic ways of coping with potentially dangerous situations in psychotic and non-psychotic populations. *Group Psychotherapy and Psychodrama, 25*(1–2), 57–68.

Moreno, J. L. (1958). Rules and techniques of psychodrama. In Jules H. Masserman and J. L. Moreno (Eds.), *Progress in psychotherapy* (Vol. 3, pp. 86–132). New York: Grune & Stratton.

Moreno, Zerka T. (1959). A survey of psychodramatic techniques. *Group Psychotherapy, 12*, 5–14.

Moreno, Zerka T. (1966). Psychodramatic rules, techniques, and adjunctive methods. *Group Psychotherapy, 18,* 73–86.

Ossorio, Abel G., & Fine, Leon. (1960). Psychodrama as a catalyst for social change in a mental hospital. In J. Masserman & J. L. Moreno (Eds.), *Progress in psychotherapy* (Vol.5)(pp.121–131). New York: Grune & Stratton.

Parrish, Marguerite. (1953). Psychodrama: Description of applications and review of techniques. *Group Psychotherapy, 6*(1–2), 74–77.

Remer, Rory. (1986). Use of psychodramatic intervention with families: Change on multiple levels. *Journal of Group Psychotherapy, Psychodrama, & Sociometry, 39*(1), 13–30.

Sacks, James M. (1967). The judgment technique in psychodrama. *Group Psychotherapy, 18*(1–2), 69–72.

Sacks, James M. (1970). The reformed auxiliary ego technique: A psychodramatic rekindling of hope. *Group Psychotherapy, 23,* 118–126.

Sacks, James M. (1970). The letter. *Group Psychotherapy and Psychodrama, 27*(3–4), 184–190.

Samuels, Mike, & Samuels, Nancy. (1975). *Seeing with the mind's eye: The history, techniques and uses of visualization.* New York: Random House/The Bookworks.

Schutz, Will. (1971). *Here comes everybody.* New York: Harper & Row.

Seabourne, Barbara. (1963). The action sociogram. *Group Psychotherapy, 16*(3), 145–155.

Seabourne, Barbara. (1985). *Practical aspects of psychodrama.* St. Louis: Author. (Originally published 1966. See Bibliography.)

Siroka, Robert, & Schloss, Gilbert A. (1968). The death scene in psychodrama. *Psychotherapy: Theory, Research, and Practice, 5,* 355–361.

Speros, Tom. (1972). The final empty chair. *Group Psychotherapy, 25*(1–2), 32–33.

Torrance, E. Paul. (1978). Sociodrama and the creative process. In Frederick Flach (Ed.), *Geigy Series on Creative Psychiatry.* Ardsley, NY: Geigy Pharmaceuticals.

Vander May, James. (1981). *Psychodrama a deux.* Grand Rapids, MI: Author.

Weiner, Hannah B., & Sacks, James M. (1969). Warm-up and sum-up. *Group Psychotherapy, 22*(1–2), 85–102.

Weiner, Hannah B., & Sacks, James M. (1981). Return from "Splendid isolation." In Richard Courtney & Gertrud Schattner (Eds.), *Drama in Therapy* (Vol. 2, pp.129–156). New York: Drama Book Specialists.

Yablonsky, Lewis. (1954). The future-projection technique. *Group Psychotherapy, 7*(3–4), 303–305.

Bibliography

In addition to the references previously presented throughout this book, there are others worthy of note. Most of the psychodrama literature is to be found in the journal of the ASGPP, called *Journal of Group Psychotherapy, Psychodrama, and Sociometry* (JGPPS). Actually, its name changed several times. Until his death, these and similar journals were published by Moreno's own Beacon House, and their various titles are listed below under his name. Since about 1980 the JGPPS has been published by Heldref, Inc. (see below). The following references emphasize the major books, as well as some additional publications that may not be widely known because they are relatively recent. Note that many references in psychodrama may be found in the books by Blatner, Corsini, Gendron, Greer, Kipper, and Swink.

Anderson, Walt. (1977). *Therapy and the arts.* New York: Harper/Colophon.
Anzieu, Didier. (1982). Psychodrama as a technique of the psycho-analysis of institutions. In Malcolm Pines & Lise Rafaelsen (Eds.), *The individual and the group* (Vol. 1). New York: Plenum. (Author's note: This book also contains other articles on psychodrama.)
Aveline, Mark. (1979, July). Action techniques in psychotherapy. *British Journal*

of Hospital Medicine, pp. 78–84.

Bischof, Ledford J. (1964). *Interpreting personality theories.* New York: Harper & Row.

Blatner, Adam. (1973). *Acting-in: Practical applications of psychodramatic methods.* New York: Springer Publishing Co. (Author's note: This paperbound book is the best introduction to the field.)

Blatner, Adam. (1985). *Creating your living: Applications of psychodramatic methods in everyday life.* San Marcos, TX: Author.

Blatner, Adam. (1988). Psychodrama. In R. J. Corsini & D. Wedding (Eds.), *Current psychotherapies* (4th ed.). Itasca, IL: Peacock.

Blatner, Adam & Blatner, Allee. (1987). *The art of play: An adult's guide to reclaiming imagination and spontaneity.* New York: Human Sciences Press.

Boies, Karen G. (1973). Role playing as a behavior change technique: Review of the empirical literature. In Isaac M. Marks (Ed.), *Psychotherapy and behavior change, 1972.* Chicago: Aldine.

Boria, Giovanni. (1983). *Tele: Manuale di psicodramma classico* [Tele: Manual of classical psychodrama]. Milan, Italy: Franco Angeli.

Buchanan, Dale R. (1984). Moreno's social atom: A diagnostic and treatment tool for exploring interpersonal relationships. *The Arts in Psychotherapy, 11,* 155–164.

Buchanan, Dale R. (1984). Psychodrama. In Tokasz B. Karasu (Ed.), *The psychiatric therapies: Part 2. The psychosocial therapies* (chap. 18). Washington, DC: American Psychiatric Association. (Author's note: This is an excellent brief summary of the subject.)

Cohen, Roberta G., & Lipkin, Gladys B. (1979). *Therapeutic group work for health professionals* (pp. 179–217). New York: Springer Publishing Co.

Compernolle, T. (1981). J. L. Moreno: An unrecognized pioneer of family therapy. *Family Process, 20,* 331–335.

Corsini, Raymond J. (1967). *Role playing in psychotherapy.* Chicago: Aldine. (Author's note: Very good, with annotated bibliography.)

Corsini, Raymond J., & Putzey, L. J. (1956). The historic background of group psychotherapy. *Group Psychotherapy, 9,* 177–249. (Author's note: A 1,700-item bibliography, including items dating from 1906 to 1955.)

Emunah, Renee. (1983). Drama therapy with adult psychiatric patients. *The Arts in Psychotherapy, 10,* 77–84.

Fine, Leon J. (1978). Psychodrama. In Raymond J. Corsini (Ed.), *Current psychotherapies* (2nd ed.). Itasca, IL: F. E. Peacock.

Fleshman, Bob, & Fryrear, Jerry. (1981). *The arts in therapy.* Chicago: Nelson-Hall. (Author's note: Excellent review of the various expressive therapies.)

Fox, Jonathan (Ed.). (1987). *The essential Moreno: Writings on psychodrama, group method, and spontaneity by J. L. Moreno.* New York: Springer Publishing Co.

Garvey, Dale M. (1967). Simulation, role-playing, and sociodrama in the social studies (with annotated bibliography). *Emporia State Research Studies, 16*(2), 5–34.

Gendron, Jeanine. (1980). *Moreno: The roots and the branches; and bibliography of psychodrama, 1972–1980.* Beacon, NY: Beacon House.

Goldman, Elaine Eller, & Morrison, Delcy Schram. (1984). *Psychodrama: Experience and process.* Phoenix, AZ: Eldemar. (5812 N. 12th St. No. 32, Phoenix, AZ 85014)

Greenberg, Ira A. (Ed.). (1974). *Psychodrama; Theory and therapy.* New York: Behavioral Publications.

Greenberg, Ira A. (Ed.). (1977). *Group hypnotherapy and hypnodrama* (pp. 231–303). Chicago: Nelson-Hall.

Greenberg, Ira A. (1986). Psychodrama. In I. L. Kutash & A Wolf (Eds.), *Psychotherapist's casebook* (chap. 24). San Francisco: Jossey-Bass.

Greer, Valerie J., & Sacks, James M. (1973). *Bibliography of psychodrama (1920–1972).* New York: Authors. (Author's note: 834 items.)

Gregoric, Linda, & Gregoric, Michael. (1981). Sociodrama: Video in social action. In J. L. Fryrear & B. Fleshman (Eds.), *Videotherapy in mental health* (pp. 244–256). Springfield, IL: Charles C. Thomas.

Hale, Ann E. (1985). *Conducting clinical sociometric explorations: A manual for psychodramatists and sociometrists.* Roanoke, VA: Author. (Royal Publishing Company, 137 W. Campbell Avenue, Roanoke, VA 24011. Author's note: This is the best introduction to the method.)

Hare, A. Paul. (1985). *Social interaction as drama.* Beverly Hills, CA: Sage Publications.

Hare, A. Paul. (1987). Bibliography of the work of J. L. Moreno. *Journal of Group Psychotherapy, Psychodrama, and Sociometry, 39*(1), 95–128.

Hawley, Robert C. (1975). *Value exploration through role playing: Practical strategies for use in the classroom.* New York: Hart.

Heisey, Marion J. (1982). *Clinical case studies in psychodrama.* Washington, DC: University Press of America.

Hudgins, M. Katherine, & Kiesler, Donald J. (1984). *Instructional manual for doubling in individual psychotherapy.* Richmond, VA: Author. (Available from Dr. D. J. Kiesler, Dept. of Psychology, Virginia Commonwealth University, 806 Franklin St., Richmond, VA 23284.)

Irwin, Eleanor C., & Portner, Elaine. (Eds.). (1984). *The scope of drama therapy: Proceedings from the first annual drama therapy conference.* New Haven, CT: Author. (Available from the NADT, 19 Edwards Street, New Haven, CT 06511.)

Jeammet, Philippe, & Kestemberg, Evelyne. (1981). Le psychodrame psychanalytique; Technique, specificité, indications. *Psychotherapies, 92*(2), 85–92.

Jeammet, Philippe, & Kestemberg, Evelyne. (1983). Le psychodrame psychanalytique a l'adolescence. *Adolescence, 1*(1), 147–163.

Jennings, Sue. (1974). *Remedial drama.* New York: Theatre Arts Books.

Jennings, Sue. (1986). *Creative drama in group work.* London: Winslow Press. (Author's note: Many useful techniques.)

Kase-Polisini, Judith. (Ed.). (1985). *Creative drama in a developmental context.* Lanham, MD: University Press of America.

Kipper, David A. (1986). *Psychotherapy through clinical role playing.* New York:

Brunner/Mazel. (Author's note: Excellent and thorough text.)

Kumar, V. K., & Treadwell, T. W. (1985). *Practical sociometry for psychodramatists.* West Chester, PA: Authors. (Dept. of Psychology, West Chester University, West Chester, PA 19383.)

Landy, Robert J. (1982). *Handbook of educational drama and theater.* Westport, CT: Greenwood Press. (Author's note: Many references on creative dramatics in education.)

Landy, Robert J. (1986). *Drama therapy: Concepts and practices.* Springfield, IL: Charles C. Thomas.

Langley, Dorothy, & Langley, Gordon E. (1983). *Dramatherapy and psychiatry.* London: Croom Helm.

Lebovici, Serge. (1974). A combination of psychodrama and psycho-analysis. In Stefan de Schill (Ed.), *The challenge for group psychotherapy: Present and future* (pp. 286–315). New York: International Universities Press.

Lee, Richard H. (1981). Video as adjunct to psychodrama and role playing. In J. L. Fryrear & B. Fleshman (Eds.), *Videotherapy in mental health* (pp. 121–145). Springfield, IL: Charles C. Thomas.

Leveton, Eva. (1977). *Psychodrama for the timid clinician.* New York: Springer Publishing Co.

Leveton, E. (1984). *Adolescent crisis* (pp. 77–97). New York: Springer Publishing Co.

McCrie, E. (1975, December). Psychodrama: An interview with Zerka T. Moreno. *Practical Psychology for Physicians,* pp. 45–48, 68–79.

McNiff, Shaun. (1981). *The arts and psychotherapy.* Springfield, IL: Charles C. Thomas.

McNiff, Shaun. (1986). *Educating the creative arts therapist: A profile of the profession.* Springfield, IL: Charles C. Thomas.

Moreno, J. L.: See Major Writings at end of this section.

Moreno, Zerka T. (1978). Psychodrama. In H. Mullan & M. Rosenbaum (Eds.), *Group psychotherapy: Theory and practice* (2nd ed.) (pp. 352–376). New York: Free Press.

Moreno, Zerka T. (1983). In H. I. Kaplan & B. J. Sadock (Eds.), *Comprehensive group psychotherapy* (2nd ed.) (pp. 158–166). Baltimore: Williams and Wilkins.

Moreno, Zerka T. (1987). Psychodrama. In Jeffrey Zeig (Ed.), *The evolution of psychotherapy* (pp. 341—358). New York: Brunner/Mazel.

Naar, Ray. (1982). *A primer of group psychotherapy* (pp. 177–203). New York: Human Sciences Press.

Nicholas, Mary W. (1984). *Change in the context of group therapy.* New York: Brunner/Mazel. (Author's note: This book includes some good theory about how psychodrama may be integrated with other modern therapies and psychologies.)

Olsson, Peter A., & Barth, Patricia A. (1983). New uses of psychodrama. *Journal of Operational Psychiatry, 14*(2), 95–101.

Petzold, Hilarion. (Ed.). (1985). *Dramatische therapie* [Drama therapy]. Stuttgart: Hippokrates Verlag. (Author's note: Contains many references to articles in

German and French.)

Petzold, Hilarion, & Mathias, U. (1982). *Rollenentwicklung und Identität* [Role development and identity]. Paderborn, Germany: Junfermann.

Polansky, Norman A. (1982). Ego functions in psychodrama. In N. Polansky (Ed.), *Integrated ego psychology* (chap. 11). New York: Aldine.

Quell, Brin. (1980). *Get those people moving: A handbook on using creative dramatics in a variety of settings*. Albany, NY: Dept. of Human Resources. (Albany City Arts Office, 450 Madison Ave., Albany NY 12210.)

Sacks, James M. (1974). The psychodramatic approach. In Donald S. Milman & George D. Goldman (Eds.), *Group process today: Evaluation and perspectives*. Springfield, IL: Charles C. Thomas.

Sacks, James H. (1981). Drama therapy with the acting out patient. In G. Schattner & R. Courtney (Eds.), *Drama in therapy: Vol. 2. Adults* (pp. 35–56.). New York: Drama Book Specialists.

Schattner, Gertrud, & Courtney, Richard. (Eds.). (1981). *Drama in therapy: Vol. 1. Children; Vol. 2. Adults*. New York: Drama Book Specialists. (Author's note: Excellent anthology with many relevant articles.)

Schramski, Thomas (1982). *A systematic model of psychodrama*. Tucson, AZ: Author. (Monograph available from author, 927 North 10th Ave., Suite A, Tucson, AZ 85705.)

Schramski, Thomas, & Feldman, Clyde A. (1984). *Selected abstracts of outcome research in the action methods*. Tucson, AZ: Author. (Obtainable from author, 927 North 10th Ave., Suite A, Tucson, AZ 85705.)

Seabourne, Barbara. (1985). *Practical aspects of psychodrama*. St. Louis: Author. (Available from the author at 546 Oakwood, St. Louis, Missouri 63119. Author's note: This 68-page monograph contains several practical papers that had been part of Blatner's 1970 publication, q.v.)

Shaftel, Fannie, & Shaftel, George. (1982). *Role-playing in the curriculum* (2nd ed.). Englewood Cliffs, NJ: Prentice-Hall. (Author's note: This is a revised edition of their 1967 book, *Role playing for social values*.)

Shaw, Malcom E., Corsini, Raymond, Blake, Robert, & Mouton, Jane. (1980). *Role playing: A practical manual for group facilitators*. San Diego, CA: University Associates. (Author's note: Excellent bibliography, oriented mainly to business and organizational audiences.)

Starr, Adeline. (1977). *Psychodrama: Rehearsal for living*. Chicago: Nelson-Hall.

Swink, David F. (1984). *Intensive psychodrama training series*. Washington, DC: St. Elizabeth's Hospital, Psychodrama Section. (Author's note: Excellent bibliography and a curriculum for training.)

Torrance, E. Paul. (1978). Sociodrama and the creative process. In Frederic Flach (Ed.), *Creative psychiatry*. (No. 14) (pp. 1–31). Ardsley, NY: Geigy Pharmaceuticals.

Torrance, E. Paul, Murdock, Mary, & Fletcher, David. (in press). *Sociodrama: Creative problem solving in action*. Buffalo, NY: Bearly, Ltd.

Treadwell, Thomas W. (Ed.). (1974). *Confrontation and training via the group process—the action techniques*. New York: Simon & Schuster. (Selected Academic Readings.)

Vander May, James H. (1981). *Psychodrama a deux.* Grand Rapids, MI: Author. (Monograph available from author at Pine Rest Christian Hospital, 300 68th Street S., Grand Rapids, MI 49508.)

Van Mentz, Morry. (1983). *The effective use of role-play: A handbook for teachers and trainers.* London: Kogan Page.

Warner, G. Douglas. (1978–1985). *Psychodrama training tips* (Vols. 1, 2). Hagerstown, MD: Author. (326 Summit Ave., Hagerstown, MD 21740.)

Weiner, Hannah B. (1975). Living experiences with death—a journeyman's view through psychodrama. *Omega, 6*(3), 251–274. (Author's note: Variety of techniques.)

Weiner, Hannah B. & Sacks, James M. (1981). Return from splendid isolation. In G. Schattner & R. Courtney (Eds.), *Drama in therapy* (pp. 129–156). New York: Drama Book Specialists.

Wolberg, Arlene R. (1976). The contributions of Jacob Moreno. In Lewis R. Wolberg & M. L. Aronson (Eds.), *Group therapy, 1976—an overview.* New York: Stratton Intercontinental Medical Books. (Author's note: Includes other relevant articles.)

Yablonsky, Lewis. (1975). *Psychodrama: Resolving emotional problems through role-playing.* New York: Basic Books.

MAJOR WRITINGS OF J. L. MORENO

This section includes some of the major writings of J. L. Moreno. The originator of psychodrama and a prolific author, he wrote many books and articles, which may be found as references in the other key items in this bibliography, especially in Hare's article and Blatner's and Gendron's books. Moreno published most of his writings in his own publishing house, Beacon House, Inc., located at his home in Beacon, New York. Except when otherwise noted, this is the publishing source of the referenced items. The sale of his remaining books has been taken over by the Horsham Clinic, and they may be obtained by writing to Beacon House, Inc., Welsh Rd. & Butler Pike, Ambler PA 19002.

Moreno, J. L. (1921). *The words of the Father.* Reissued in 1971. (Author's note: First published anonymously in Vienna; inspirational poetry and some exposition of Moreno's philosophical–theological ideas. Also entitled *The psychodrama of God: A new hypothesis of the self.*)

Moreno, J. L. (1923). *The theater of spontaneity.* (Author's note: First published in Vienna with the title *Das Stegreiftheatre*; translated and published by Beacon House in 1947 and 1972.)

Moreno, J. L. (1934). *Who shall survive? A new approach to the problem of human interrelations.* Washington, DC: Nervous & Mental Disease Publishing Co. (Author's note: In 1953, this was revised and expanded and the subtitle changed, to *Who shall survive? Foundations of sociometry, group psychotherapy, and sociodrama.*)

Moreno, J. L. (1946). *Psychodrama* (Vol. 1). (Republished 1972.)

Moreno, J. L. (1951). (Ed.). *Sociometry: Experimental method and the science of society.*

Moreno, J. L. (1956). *Sociometry and the science of man.*

Moreno, J. L. (1956–1960). (Ed.), *Progress in psychotherapy* (Vols. 1–5). New York: Grune & Stratton. (Vol. 1 co-edited with Frieda Fromm-Reichman; Vols. 2–5, with Jules Masserman; both were the first names on the books.)

Moreno, J. L. (1960). *The Sociometry Reader.* Glencoe, IL: The Free Press. (Co-edited with Helen Hall Jennings and others.)

Moreno, J. L. (1969). *Psychodrama* (Vol. 3).

Moreno, J. L. (1971). Psychodrama. In H. I. Kaplan & B. Sadock (Eds.), *Comprehensive group psychotherapy.* Baltimore: Williams and Wilkins.

Moreno, J. L. (1972). The religion of God-Father. In Paul E. Johnson (Ed.), *Healer of the mind: A psychiatrist's search for faith.* Nashville, TN: Abingdon.

Moreno, J. L., & Elefthery, Dean G. (1975). An introduction to group psychodrama. In George Gazda (Ed.), *Basic approaches to group psychotherapy and group counseling* (2nd ed.). Springfield, IL: Charles C. Thomas.

Moreno, J. L., Friedemann, A., Battegay, R., & Moreno, Z. (Eds.) (1966). *International handbook of group psychotherapy.* New York: Philosophical Library.

Moreno, J. L., & Moreno, Z. T. (1956). *Psychodrama* (Vol. 2).

Journals edited and/or published by Dr. Moreno:

Sociometry: A Journal of Interpersonal Relations (Vols. 1–18, 1937–1956). (Author's note: The early volumes contain some of Moreno's basic ideas and reflect the eclecticism of the people whose works were published in them. In 1956, this journal was turned over to the American Sociological Society.)

International Journal of Sociometry (Vols. 1–5, 1956–1968).

Handbook of International Sociometry (Vols. 6–8, 1971–1973).

Sociatry (Vols. 1–3, 1947–1950).

Group Psychotherapy (Vols. 4–22, 1951–1970). (Continuation, with title change, of *Sociatry.*)

Group Psychotherapy and Psychodrama (Vols. 23–28, 1970–1975). (Continuation, with title change, of *Group Psychotherapy.*)

[Following Moreno's death in 1974, the journal continued, edited by a committee of leaders in the field of psychodrama.]

Group Psychotherapy, Psychodrama, and Sociometry (Vols. 29–33, 1976–1980).

The Journal of Group Psychotherapy, Psychodrama, and Sociometry (Vol. 34+,

1980–present). (Published by Heldref Publications, 4000 Albemarle Street, NW, Washington, DC 20016, under the editorship of the American Society for Group Psychotherapy and Psychodrama.)

Appendix A: A Historical Chronology of Psychodrama and Group Psychotherapy

EARLY PIONEERS

1905: Joseph H. Pratt, an internist at Massachusetts General Hospital in Boston, offered inspirational lectures to patients with tuberculosis. He gathered his patients into groups and explained to them the necessity of hygienic instructions and exhorted them to be submissive to his will. This "classroom method" was descriptively called "thought control," and other doctors employed the same method in a variety of physical disorders (Pratt, 1907). Later, in the 1920s and 1930s, Pratt gave informational talks to psychiatric patients at the Boston Dispensary in which he placed less emphasis on the disease and more on the emotions and their effect on psychoneuroses. The group became for him the focal point of therapy (Pratt, 1945).

1908–1911: Jacob L. Moreno began to experiment with creative drama with children in Vienna.

1912: Moreno organized the first self-help group, with the disadvantaged class of prostitutes in Vienna.

1917–1918: Moreno worked with Tyrolean refugees of World War I who were relocated to a camp on the outskirts of Vienna; here he developed his earliest ideas about sociometry.

1921: E. W. Lazell worked with World War I veterans at St. Elizabeth's Hospital in Washington, DC. His procedure was similar to Pratt's, but he worked with mentally ill patients and called his lectures to the patients on psychoanalytic dynamics "group analysis" (Lazell, 1921).

1921: Alfred Adler and Rudolph Dreikurs in Vienna held case conferences with teachers, families, and the child or teenager all together and did some of their counseling in these settings. Later, Dreikurs worked with groups of alcoholics in Vienna before coming to the United States.

1921–1924: J. L. Moreno organized his "Theatre of Spontaneity" in Vienna, the beginning of what was to become psychodrama. (Moreno set the date of April 1, 1921 as the "official" beginning of psychodrama.) In 1923 he published *Das Stegreiftheatre* (the Theatre of Spontaneity), in which he wrote about ideas regarding spontaneity research, role theory, and action studies. He also designed the first theater-in-the-round (Held, 1982). Moreno considered the period from 1911 to 1923 the first "axionormative" period, the time when the basic philosophical foundations were laid in the development of sociometric theory (Renouvier, 1958).

1922: Sigmund Freud speculated on group dynamics in his paper "Group Psychology and the Analysis of the Ego."

1923–1930: Trigant Burrow worked intensively with some experimental groups and (beginning in 1918) used psychoanalytic methods in the group setting. He used the group to reduce the authority of the analyst and developed some interesting social theories of behavior.

1927–1929: J. L. Moreno demonstrated role playing at Mt. Sinai Hospital in New York (and elsewhere).

1929: Louis Wender began to do group work that was psychoanalytically oriented (Wender, 1951).

1929–1930: L. Cody Marsh, a minister at Kings Park State Hospital in New York, brought a revivalist-style spirit to the task of helping his patients: "By the crowd they have been broken, by the crowd shall they be healed." He broadcast inspirational talks and instituted ideas of "milieu treatment." He considered each patient to be a student who received his "condition" as part of learning about "the great subject of civilization" and who needed to experience being "reeducated" (Marsh, 1931). During this period, Austin Riggs also lectured over loudspeakers to psychiatric patients in a Stockbridge, Massachusetts, hospital.

1929–1930: Moreno offered Impromptu Theater, combining psychodrama and group dynamics, at Carnegie Hall.

1931: Moreno consulted as a psychiatrist at Sing Sing prison in New York and began to write about the use of group psychotherapy.

1932: J. L. Moreno first coined the terms "group therapy" and "group psychotherapy" at a conference of the American Psychiatric Association in Philadelphia, after doing basic research on prison populations. (He was encouraged to do this work by William Alanson White.) Moreno's approach of truly interactional, group-centered methods was in contrast to earlier group methods that were often classes in mental health, taught by lecture and exhortation.

1933: Moreno consulted at the New York State Training School for Girls in Hudson, New York, in collaboration with Helen Hall Jennings; and over the next several years he introduced role playing and worked out his sociometric system. On April 4, he exhibited some of his early charts at the New York Medical Society convention; he considered this the official start of the "sociometric movement."

1934: Moreno published *Who Shall Survive—A New Approach to the Problem of Human Interrelations*. He also introduced psychodrama at St. Elizabeth's Hospital in Washington, DC, which was one of the most dynamic psychiatric centers in the country at the time. He received a good deal of support from many of the leaders in the profession.

1934: Samuel R. Slavson, an engineer volunteering with the Jewish Board of Guardians' Big Sister Program, began to do volunteer arts and crafts activities with groups of teenage girls in group homes. He went on to become allied to psychoanalysis and began to expand his activities, calling it "ego therapy" and applying it to groups of latency age and finally even preschool children. He considered his work "para-analytic," and it involved generally permissive play therapy and lectures.

1934: Paul Schilder at Bellevue Hospital in New York organized psychoanalytically oriented groups for both inpatients and outpatients. In these, he would interpret both resistance and transference phenomena.

1936: Moreno opened Beacon Hill Sanitarium, a private psychiatric hospital about 60 miles north of New York City on the Hudson River, with an attached psychodrama theater and facilities for training professionals. (This is also the year he became a naturalized citizen.)

1937: Moreno began the publication of his first professional journal, *Sociometry: A Journal of Interpersonal Relations.* (He used the term "interpersonal relations" before it became the name of the approach used by Harry Stack Sullivan.) He applied sociometric testing procedures to Public School 181 in Brooklyn. Moreno considered this year the beginning of the "second sociometric phase."

1937: Lauretta Bender (Schilder's wife and a major pioneer in child psychiatry), also at Bellevue, organized play therapy groups with emotionally disturbed children (Bender, 1937).

1936–1937: Kurt Lewin, Muzafer Sharif, and other social psychologists began important studies in group dynamics, although it was not oriented to therapy.

1937: Abraham A. Low, in Chicago, used "will training" in his work with the mentally ill; later, in 1941, he organized Recovery, Inc., a self-help group program that used discussion and the reading of selected books of his as an aftercare program.

1937: Alcoholics Anonymous, started a few years earlier in Akron, Ohio, was beginning to be recognized.

1940: S. H. Foulkes and E. James Anthony organized the Group Analytic Society in Northfield, England.

THE PERIOD OF EXPANSION

1941: A psychodrama theater was built and put into operation at St. Elizabeth's Hospital in Washington, DC.

1941–1945: During World War II, group therapy began to be used widely in military and veterans' hospitals.

1942: J. L. Moreno organized the American Society for Group Psychotherapy and Psychodrama (ASGPP), the first professional association for group therapists. He also opened the Sociometric Institute and Theater of Psychodrama at 101 Park Avenue in New York City and began to offer open sessions, attracting many curious professionals from a variety of disciplines. This was the beginning of what he considered the "third phase of sociometric development," which was followed by the spread of group psychotherapy, sociometry, and psychodrama, nationally and internationally. (Moreno's open sessions continued on weekend nights until the early 1970s. In 1962, he moved this "storefront setting" to 236 West 78th Street.)

1943: S. R. Slavson founded the American Group Psychotherapy Association, which was oriented toward psychoanalytic practice. He also began publishing *The International Journal of Group Psychotherapy.*

1945: Moreno began publication of his second journal, *Sociatry,* which later became the official professional organ of the ASGPP and after 2 years was renamed *Group Psychotherapy.* The next year he published *Psychodrama* (Volume 1) (Corsini & Putzey, 1956). Many other books and articles followed, as noted in the Bibliography.

1946–1949: A. Snedeker, as Surgeon-General, instituted a policy to make group psychotherapy the principal form of psychiatric treatment in Veterans Administration hospitals.

1946–1950: J. D. Sutherland, S. H. Foulkes, and H. Ezriel applied psychoanalysis in groups at the Tavistock Clinic in London. Winifred Bion, a follower of Melanie Klein, began to research group culture. This group began publication of a journal, *Human Relations—A Journal of Small Group Research.*

1946: Joshua Bierer, in England, had integrated Adlerian ideas and written about group work and social psychiatry since 1938. He created social clubs for recovering patients.

1946–1947: Nathan Ackerman began to write about his early use of conjoint group methods in dealing with families.

1946–1947: The National Training Laboratories at Bethel, Maine, began their community development conferences, which later evolved into the T-group and then the encounter group. Several of the leaders had been students of Kurt Lewin and J. L. Moreno.

The key figures were Ronald Lippitt, Kenneth Benne, Leland Bradford, and Jack Gibb (Gottschalk & Pattison, 1969; Lippitt, Bradford, & Benne, 1947).

1948–1949: Alexander Wolf said individual psychoanalysis could be done in a group setting, and in his writings he noted that the group context recreates patients' family dynamics in many ways.

1949: Robert Bartlett Haas applied group theories and psychodrama to educational contexts, both in the classroom and on playgrounds.

1949–1955: Maxwell Jones developed the concept of the "therapeutic community" at the Social Rehabilitation Unit (later renamed Henderson Hospital) of the Belmont Hospital in Sutton, England. Around that time, Paul Sivadon in France pioneered the idea of open (unlocked) wards.

1950–1960: Expansion of group psychotherapy, especially by such leaders as Martin Grotjahn, Hyman Spotnitz, Jerome Frank, Florence Powdermaker, Clifford Sager, Helen Papanek, Max Rosenbaum, Helen Durkin, and many others. Children were treated in groups by Haim Ginott, Gisela Konopka, Fritz Redl, and others.

1955–1959: Sensitivity training, an extension of T-group ideas, was being explored at the UCLA School of Business Administration in California and in other locations as part of the expansion of the National Training Laboratories.

THE PERIOD OF INNOVATION

1958–1966: Frederick (Fritz) Perls, Laura Perls, Paul Goodman, Ralph Hefferline, and others developed Gestalt therapy in New York; it became popular after Fritz Perls moved to the Esalen Institute in California around 1966.

1963–1966: Marathon (time-extended) group therapy (mainly for personal growth); Frederick Stoller, George Bach, Elizabeth Mintz.

1963–1966: Eric Berne developed his method of Transactional Analysis.

1963–1966: Michael Murphy and Richard Price organized Esalen Institute just south of Big Sur, California. It was the prototype of the "growth center," and hundreds sprouted up around the country (and some overseas) over the next decade. These centers became the focus of the human potential movement, which was a marriage of humanistic psychology and T-group methods.

1967: Will Schutz, at Esalen, combined many modes of therapy with the process of the basic encounter group—psychodrama, bioenergetic analysis, sensory awakening, guided fantasy, and a variety of action techniques, many of which were ultimately based on Moreno's methods.

1967: Synanon "games" opened to the public as a form of encounter group in Santa Monica, a seaside suburb on the west side of Los Angeles. Synanon was started in 1958 as a drug abuse treatment center by Charles Diedrich. These games were just short of being violently confrontational, and some of this approach generalized to contaminate parts of the encounter group movement.

1968: Hindu gurus, swamis, and Eastern spiritual teachers and disciplines were becoming fashionable, in part stimulated by the support of the Beatles for the Maharishi Mahesh Yogi and his system of transcendental meditation. The use of psychedelic agents added to metaphysical interest, and group therapies began integrating transpersonal issues.

In the 1960s, a number of other forms of psychotherapy became relatively popular, and some of these approaches were applied in group contexts: family therapy (involving several families at a time); art, movement, and other expressive therapies; Arthur Janov's primal therapy; William Glasser's reality therapy; and the like.

Around this period of aroused community action in all areas, self-help groups for smokers, eaters, gays, and gamblers; various special medical problem groups; families of reading-disabled children and mentally ill adults; and many other categories expanded the concept of group work tremendously. Hospice centers were formed and began to offer bereavement groups in the mid-1970s.

In summary, I believe the next frontier for the use of group therapy will be its natural integration into all aspects of our society, as more people develop the skills to utilize the group context to facilitate management, education, recreation, and political action.

REFERENCES

Bender, L. (1937). Group activities on a children's ward as a method of psychotherapy. *American Journal of Psychiatry, 93*, 151–173.

Corsini, Raymond J., & Putzey, J. J. (1956). Bibliography on group psychotherapy. *Group Psychotherapy, 9*(3), 177–249.

Gottschalk, Louis, & Pattison, E. Mansell. (1969). Psychiatric perspectives on T-groups and the laboratory method: An overview. *American Journal of Psychiatry, 126*(6), 824.

Held, R. L. (1982). *Endless innovations: Frederick Kreisler's theory and scenic design* (pp. 33–36). Ann Arbor, MI: UMI Research Press.

Lazell, E. W. (1921). The group treatment of dementia praecox. *Psychoanalytic Review, 8*, 168–179.

Lippitt, Ronald, Bradford, Leland P., & Benne, Kenneth D. (1947). Sociodramatic clarification of leader and group roles, as a starting point for effective group functioning. *Sociatry: A Journal of Group and Intergroup Therapy, 1*(1), 82–91. (Author's note; These and other pioneers of the T-group method also published a number of other first papers on the subject in Moreno's journals around 1947.)

Marsh, L. C. (1931). Group treatment of the psychoses by the psychological equivalent of the revival. *Mental Hygiene in New York, 15*, 328–349.

Pratt, J. H. (1907). The organization of tuberculosis classes. *Medical Communications of the Massachusetts Medical Society, 20*, 475–492.

Pratt, J. H. (1945). Group method in the treatment of psychosomatic disorders. *Sociometry, 8*, 323–331.

Renouvier, Pierre. (1958). The group psychotherapy movement and J. L. Moreno, its pioneer and founder. *Group Psychotherapy, 11*(1), 69–86.

Wender, Louis. (1951). Reflections on group psychotherapy. *Quarterly Review of Psychiatry and Neurology, 6*, 246–248.

Appendix B: A Psychodramatic Story

A Tale by Nachman of Bratzlav (c. 1820)

Once there was a prince who fell into the delusion that he was a rooster. He took off his clothes, squatted under the table, and ate only grain or crumbs. The king sent for many doctors, but none of them could cure the prince. Finally, a wise man appeared before the king and said, "I think I can heal the prince," and the king gave him permission to try.

The sage removed his clothes and, joining the prince under the table, began to munch at some grain and crow like a rooster. The prince looked at him suspiciously and asked, "Who are you and what are you doing here?" The wise man responded with the same question. The prince replied, "I am a rooster!" "Oh, really?" said the sage. "So am I!" After a while they became friends.

When the sage felt the prince had grown accustomed to his presence, he signaled for a shirt and put it on. The prince confronted him belligerently: "Are you crazy? Are you forgetting who you are? Are you trying to be a man?" The wise man replied, "You mustn't believe that a rooster who dresses like a man ceases to be a rooster." The prince thought about this for a while, and then he put a shirt on, too. After a time the sage signaled to have food put under the table. "Wretch! What are you doing?" protested the prince, "Are you going to eat like them now?" The wise man allayed his fears: "Don't be upset. A rooster can eat the food humans eat and still be a good rooster." The prince considered this for a time, and then he began to eat food.

Finally, the wise man said, "Do you think a rooster has to sit under the table all the time? He can get up and walk around if he wants to and still be a good rooster." The prince then followed the wise man up from under the table and began to walk. "Remember," the sage said, "you can do anything with man in his world and yet remain the rooster you are." The prince was convinced and resumed his life as a person.

Index

Index